Many believers wonder when God will finally reveal their calling. I've wondered this very thing myself. Even after walking the "red carpet" Teasi writes about, the question was still there waiting for me. In her inspiring and refreshingly humorous way, Teasi takes a hard question that many struggle with and simplifies the answer, giving readers new understanding, direction, and motivation to get up and get walking in truth.

Jo Dee Messina, multiplatinum-selling singer and songwriter

I have never read a book on my "calling" quite like this one! It's beyond amazing, and it may very well be the missing puzzle piece in your life that will finally begin to make all things clear. If you have ever felt hopeless, overlooked, or just plain lost in the pursuit of your calling, I urge you to read this book. I feel certain it will help guide you to a place of understanding and solid answers, as it has for me. And the beautiful thing is, you are closer than you realize.

Tammy Trent, music artist, speaker, and author of *Learning to Breathe Again*

In our Christian culture, "What's your calling?" is the new, "What are you going to be when you grow up?" question. Author Teasi Cannon reminds us that our search for "calling" can distract and even derail our walk of faith. She infuses hope that where we are right now—each and every day—can be used for God's purpose. And that knowledge alone gives me such freedom.

Joanne Kraft, speaker and author of *The Mean Mom's Guide to Raising Great Kids* and *Just Too Busy—Taking Your Family on a Radical Sabbatical*

Our friend Teasi Cannon is a gifted teacher, and this book is an incredible guide for anyone who is ready to find something far more meaningful than a calling. We pray readers will be encouraged and drawn into a deeper understanding of God's plans, just as we have been.

Jeremy and Adie Camp, husband-and-wife singers and songwriters

———

This book gently (and generously) lets you off of a mental merry-go-round you may not have even realized you were on. Written with refreshing candor and bolstered with biblical truth, Teasi Cannon's insight simultaneously lifts the fog and lights a fire. I will never again lose sleep over my calling or lose sight of my fixed purpose. Thank you, Teasi!

Toni Birdsong, author of *More than a Bucket List: Making Your Dreams, Passions, and Faith a Reality*

———

We live in a time where the drive to discover our destiny often rises above our desire for Jesus. Consumed with finding our calling, we may miss God's purpose for our lives, which is already right in front of us. Aided by adventures with vacuum cleaners, red carpets, and the little land of Amazingville, my friend Teasi Cannon provides a scriptural perspective that will keep you centered on the Person of Jesus while walking in His purposes. I highly commend Teasi and this book to you!

Dave Buehring, pastor, speaker, and author of *The Jesus Blueprint: Rediscovering His Original Plan for Changing the World*

———

Understanding the difference between your calling and your purpose is important to a fruitful walk with Jesus. Teasi's insights are simple yet profound, and written with refreshing transparency.

Nancy Reece, internal advisor for The Human Capital Group; author of *Undivided Hearts: Tender Wisdom for Tough Choices*

———

Much has been said about our calling and our purpose, yet few seem to understand the puzzling difference between them. Teasi Cannon nails it! Her work brings real clarity into one of life's biggest pursuits, and the content of this book has life-changing implications. A must-read for all who seek to understand the real meaning of their life.

Steve Craver, president of Communicate to Connect; executive coach, speaker, and trainer

As a pastor, I've seen the simple question of "What's my calling?" become a perpetual detour for too many people. Teasi Cannon brings much-needed clarity to the topic of "calling" and how it emerges in, and shapes, a Christ follower's life. This book is enormously practical for believers eager to be used by God, and for anyone looking for a clear sense of purpose and meaning in their life.

Steve Berger, pastor of Grace Chapel, Leiper's Fork, Tennessee

LORD, WHERE'S *MY* CALLING?

LORD, WHERE'S *MY* CALLING?

When the Big Question Becomes a Big Distraction

TEASI CANNON

Wheaton Press
Train. Equip. Reflect.

Lord, Where's *My* Calling?

Published in the U.S. by Wheaton Press
www.wheatonpress.com

For more books in this series, classroom and small group discounts, and other resources, visit www.wheatonpress.com.

ISBN-13: 978-0-692-48278-0
ISBN-10: 0-692-48278-4

Library of Congress Control Number: 2016921353

Cover Design: Brian Bobel
Project Manager and Editor: Kris Bearss

To Bill, my best friend

CONTENTS

INTRODUCTION

I haven't found mine yet. My special life calling, that is. As I write this, I'm nearly half-a-century old, and I just don't have the faintest clue what it is.

How about you? Do you know yours? Some of you actually might. Some people do find one pretty early on—like they've always known, maybe even in the womb. And that is truly wonderful.

But not me. And that's okay.

It hasn't always been okay, though. In fact, for years it nearly drove me crazy. I searched everywhere for it. Prayed for prophetic words. Begged God for the answer. *Please tell me, God. What is my special calling? I'm getting old . . . You're running out of time!*

He hasn't answered that question yet. At least not with the pinpoint plan I always thought would come. But what He *has* given me is even better. And it really boils down to a complete overhaul of my perspective. A beautiful about-face that has changed everything.

He has shown me my *purpose.*

What's the difference? you might be wondering. *Isn't a purpose the same as a calling?*

Well, not really. Actually, not at all from what I've found. One is all about *doing,* and the other is all about *being.* And the difference between the two has literally changed my life. I wonder if it might do the same for you, rescuing some other wanderers (and wonderers) from the depression and the ache. From that feeling of being left behind. From the fear that we turned our back for just a second too long and missed it. *Too bad; you blinked. That train is long gone!*

Um, yeah . . . that's just not true.

We haven't missed anything. We haven't been forgotten. Those of us who haven't found our special calling aren't misfits or over-looked souls. We are exactly where we're supposed to be and who we're supposed to be. And *that* truth ought not disappoint. In no way is it a concession speech for a *less than* life.

So, no, we haven't missed anything. But I do believe we've messed something up. I believe we've possibly allowed something good to become so inflated in our priorities that we've assigned it a place it was never intended to have.

For me to ask God what He's calling me to do is a good thing; I definitely want Him to lead my life, after all. But to become des-perate to discover some epic, radical, mountain-moving calling on *my* life is *not* good. In fact, if we are really honest, this pursuit has all the trappings of an idol, when a good little thing like ask-ing God for direction becomes the object of our desire.

I'll put it this way: when our desire for God's *direction* takes priority over our desire for the *Divine* Himself, we've fallen into a trap. An ugly pit filled with disappointment and despair. A place where we can work ourselves silly trying to figure out what we're doing wrong . . . or what we need to do bigger or better.

We find ourselves there because we've been lured off course by something *good*—always slightly out of reach, of course—that distracts us from what is *best*. Once we discover the incredible purpose for which we exist, however, a "special calling" becomes nothing but a *thang*. If you have one, great. If you don't . . . well, no biggie. Because, truthfully, anything God directs us to do *is* special. Including laundry. (Just try going without a washing machine for a couple of weeks, and you'll see how much it matters!) You might not be convinced just yet, and that's okay. Convincing isn't my goal. Encouraging is.

My hope for anyone who reads this book is that you would find encouragement in the pages that follow, and that you would turn the last page changed. Filled with purpose and new joy. Ready to see things differently than perhaps you have in years—or ever. Ready to take hold of what the Maker of heaven and earth has deemed yours all along.

So, if you're ready for a paradigm shift and a lot more joy, let's go. I truly believe it's possible. It's a bit like Dorothy's ruby slippers in *The Wizard of Oz*. She had those silly shoes on her feet all along. Everything she needed in order to end her crazy, desperate search for the Wizard—and ultimately for the peace and comfort of home—was with her the entire time. She just had to see it and move her heels a little.

Could it be that easy for us? I honestly think so.

CHAPTER ONE

THE EXHAUSTING SEARCH

What would you think if you saw this scene?

A young mother sits on her couch nursing a newborn while her toddler cuddles in under her free arm. Together, they listen to her home-schooled second grader read the day's story selection. As soon as she gets a moment to herself, this mom thanks God for His blessings and then asks with sincerity and anticipation: Lord, where's my calling?

Or how about this one?

A public school teacher stands before her seventh-grade language arts classes year after year, encouraging her students to be better communicators, to love literature, to do their best, and—in every way she can without losing her job—sharing her love for Jesus, hoping to leave a mark. Whenever she gets time with the Lord, she thanks Him for His grace, and asks with sincerity and longing: Lord, where's my calling?

Or this?

A woman experiences incredible healing and hope in her life, writes a book about it, and then brings that hope with her as she speaks to women's groups around the country. Countless women relate to her and feel encouraged by her testimony. In her personal prayer time, she thanks God for His love and healing, and then begs Him to answer this question: Lord, where's my calling?

I don't know about you, but when I read each of those scenarios, I feel like saying, "Woman, are you crazy?" Because what those gals are praying and looking for seems so obvious: *You're a mom! You're a teacher! You're an author! For cryin' out loud, ladies!* Those dense darlings are missing something the rest of us can so plainly see . . .

What you may have also figured out is, each of those precious little ladies is me.

Today it's quite clear that, in each of those seasons, I was doing exactly what I was called to do. But back then, I was on a desperate search for something more. Even though I loved being a mom and a teacher and an author—and of course, I knew all those roles were valuable—nothing I was doing ever felt like my *special* calling. You know, the BIG calling of my life. My red-carpet calling, handmade for me and announced by the heavenly host, complete with appropriate fanfare and full orchestra. I hate to say it, but those other things I was doing didn't really feel like . . . enough.

You're probably familiar with the kind of calling I'm talking about. You may be looking for yours even now. Most of us have been told it's *out there somewhere.* I probably run across two or three blogs a week on this topic. Books galore speak of it. Programs have been developed touting "3 easy steps" to finding it. *Step right up, folks! Anyone can access the answer!*

Well, apparently for me, that "3" needs several zeros behind it, because I have yet to complete the program. And that's just fine. It turns out the program—the find-your-calling program—isn't the one God wanted me to sign up for to begin with. He had a different plan for me. A simpler and more glorious plan. And, funny enough, I used to know that. I knew what life was about. I had my sights set right on Jesus, and He was alright with me (shout out to the Doobie Brothers).

Somewhere along the way, I guess I got distracted.

ALONG THE WAY

Were you a complete mess before you met Jesus? I definitely was. Some people are just a little lost before they find their way, but I was *really, really* lost. I can remember many empty nights, looking up into the southern California sky, wondering what it was all about. *It . . .* you know . . . LIFE. Why was I even alive? Did anything matter?

I lived with that question floating around between my ears for years. And I felt hopeless—like there was a huge hole inside of me. So what did I do? I attempted to fill it in all the wrong ways. Those blasted wrong ways.

Looking back, I can so easily see that I was aching to believe my life had a *purpose*. That I was alive for a reason. That everything I was going through mattered. That I wasn't all alone in a meaningless story that would inevitably end in a pine box.

And then Jesus came.

He saved me. And He told me something absolutely mind-blowing: *Teasi, your life matters.*

Not only did it matter, but I learned I was part of a BIG story. I was actually planned before the beginning of time to be a part of a beautiful story about this guy named Jesus who came to earth to save everyone who would believe in Him.

He was the main character. The story was ALL about *Him*. *His* life. *His* death. *His* resurrection. *His* glorious victory. *His* desire to save and heal and bring hope. And I was thrilled to be given an incredible supporting role in this fabulous work.

I understood that my *purpose* was to grow closer to this Jesus— to learn all about Him and make Him famous. And I could not have been more excited about anything. I was in love. Literally positioned—totally secure—in God's love. I needed nothing else.

Until . . . I needed something else.

It didn't come suddenly, this need. No, it made its way very, very gradually into my life. At first it was just a little thing. Just a sweet little prayer that couldn't hurt a flea: *Father, what do You want me to do with my life?*

See? Absolutely nothing wrong with that, right? Even Jesus asked this. One need only read John's Gospel—just that one—in order to plainly see Jesus saying over and over again that He only did what the Father told Him to do.

I simply wanted to be like Jesus.

And when it all started (the gradual departure from simplicity, that is), I really *did* want to do something great for God. My desire was fueled by my great love for HIM. He had loved me so much and saved me from so much, it was only natural to want to reciprocate and do something for Him. *Anything You ask, Father. Here I am. Send me.*

And He did. He sent me straight to the hospital to give birth to a few babies and then spend years wiping their bottoms and losing hours of sleep. Of course, it was far sweeter than that in reality—many moments of cuddles and kisses that I desperately wish I could get back, even if only for a second. But back then it was just a bit shocking. I mean, I had been so willing to go *anywhere*, and this was the plan? Not Africa or Washington DC or even downtown Nashville? No. He sent me to my suburban home in Franklin, Tennessee.

Yee haw.

A GROWING PROBLEM

Like a cute, tiny baby, my innocent little prayer began to grow and change over time. What started as a simple desire to bless God for the things He had done for me, slowly became a search for a cool *calling*.

LORD, WHERE'S *MY* CALLING?

Everyone around me seemed to have one. Or if they didn't have it yet, it was well on its way. The signs were plain as day for all to see! Doors flying open left and right . . . for others! Opportunity calling on seemingly everyone . . . except me. Apparently, opportunity had lost my number.

No worries, I was told. I just needed to take some time to figure out my spiritual gifts and jot down my talents and interests. Once I had all those ingredients . . . then mix together, say a prayer over them, and *voila!* Out would come my special calling.

This would have been fantastic except I didn't really know what my spiritual gifts were. And, quite honestly, I've never been super-talented at anything in particular. I'm not trying to have a pity party here; I'm just stating a fact. I am capable at many things. I am a genuine combination of administrative ability, communication skills, and basic creativity. But I'm not stand-out-above-the-rest amazing at anything. It was just plain depressing. *God, why did You make me so bland? So . . . nondescript?*

Since fusing obscure spiritual gifts with ambiguous talents and passions doesn't give a gal much to go on, I began to look around for the answer. And I'm pretty sure that's when my heart started taking the turn. Not a hard left or right; just a slight veer, undetectable because the words still sounded the same: *Father, what do You want me to do with my life?* Beneath the surface, however, the emphasis was slowly changing. It started looking a bit more like this: *Father, what do You want ME to do with MY life?*

Inch by inch it was becoming less about Him (you know, the One about whom the BIG story is written) and more about little ol' me. *Skootch over just a little, God, would ya?*

CAN ANYONE TELL ME?

So, as I said, I began to look around to see if God would reveal my calling in a different way. Maybe I couldn't figure it out because He had something special up His sleeve just for me. Yes, that had to be it!

I had heard of things like this happening. You probably have too . . . *A woman is just minding her own business at the grocery when, out of the blue, a stranger approaches with a word from the Lord: "God sent me over here to tell you that He wants you to sell it all and head straight back to Wyoming. You will start a church with your husband, and many will be saved because of your selfless sacrifice." The freshly anointed one grabs one more bag of chips with tears streaming down her face because she knows exactly what it means. It's her special calling!*

The grocery was evidently not the venue for me, though, because the only time a stranger ever approached me was to ask where the baking soda was shelved. Still, I wasn't deterred. There were plenty of other options, especially since the most Creative One had devised the master plan!

Maybe it was going to be a billboard on the freeway? *A guy is driving along, looks up at just the right moment before taking his exit, and sees that prophetic word in larger-than-life lettering—REFRESHING—and instantly he knows. He's been seeing the word everywhere, and in his quiet time, God has told him, "I've called you to bring refreshing to the nations." He will travel the world, visiting the downcast and bringing them the living water. Yes, this is it, the confirmation he's been looking for! He knows without a doubt: it's his special calling!*

I looked and looked at billboards for years, but nothing. Nada. *Not gonna be billboards for me either, I guess.*

Maybe a conference? Surely I would find it there. Maybe God would put it on the heart of the speaker right in the middle of the sermon. That would be cool!

Nope. Not that either. I can't tell you how many times I saw people singled out by a speaker for a personalized message straight from above. How incredible. How fun. But . . . it wasn't my time.

What about me? Hello, God?

Over the years this once-innocent question grew so big, so important, that it began to occupy more and more space in my prayer life. I'm not kidding when I say that I asked God to give me something—a sign, a word, a butterfly, anything—several times a day! I also subscribed to prophetic newsletters. I asked those farther along in the faith for any kind of help they could give me. And yes, I even opened fortune cookies (sanctified unto the Lord first, of course), hoping for a sign.

It got so bad that every time my sweet husband would call from work, I would hold my breath, waiting expectantly for him to tell me *it* had happened. You know, someone had stopped by his office to share a word they'd received from the Lord about *me*, containing the big clue to the answer I was desperate for.

But then, when Bill's only message was, "I just wanted you to know how much I love you . . ." I felt deflated. *That's it? You love me? Thanks, but please don't call out of the blue like that again until you can tell me what God wants me to do with my life!*

A SAD DEPARTURE

It got really bad. I lost peace. I lost joy. I really lost my way.

I was lured away by something good: a desire to do God's will. I just wanted to know what He had planned for me. I wanted Him to give me directions, to give me an answer.

To give me . . . give me . . . give me.

Ugh. That good little desire snuck up on me and grew slowly into a big, ugly distraction. A departure from what is best. And all the while my fear grew. Would I be forgotten? Would anything exciting ever happen for me, or would I end up being a boring, overlooked, secondary character in God's story—sent here merely to provide support services for the "leading men and women" with the meaningful, exciting lives?

I couldn't bear the thought of that.

My anxiety grew to where I didn't believe my life could ever truly be complete until I was finally given my very own special calling.

Boy, was I wrong! And I'm so glad I was.

HOW ABOUT YOU?

1) Where do you find glimpses of yourself in this chapter?

2) Where have you looked for your special calling?

3) How do you feel when you hear that the search for a special calling can actually become a distraction? In what ways has this been true for you?

4) "Life can be fulfilling without a special calling." What is your reaction to that statement? Does it give you joy? Anxiety? Do you disbelieve it or doubt it? Explain.

POINTS ON PURPOSE:

» There's nothing wrong with asking God to direct our steps, but we must always remember that our treasure isn't a divine roadmap; it's the Divine Himself.

» It's easy to get distracted by the lure of some great calling. Taking an honest look at our prayer life—what we're asking God for most frequently—can be a useful litmus test, revealing our true priorities as well as where we might be veering off course.

CHAPTER TWO

WEBSTER TO THE RESCUE

I'll bet you haven't heard many people credit the dictionary with saving their lives, but I'm here to tell you, good ol' Webster was used by the Lord to pick me up out of the pit.

I can remember exactly where I was—sitting in my favorite reading (and pouting) spot on the couch—when the idea occurred to me: *Look up the word* calling.

At first I thought it was a perfectly dumb idea because, of course, I already knew what a calling was. I'd been praying my guts out for it, like forever! But the thought wouldn't leave.

Look it up.

So I did. And this is what I found:

Calling: *The characteristic cry of a female cat in heat.*

Okay, that's not the definition the Lord actually used to save me, but I couldn't help myself . . . I'm the mother of teenage boys!

Seriously, the definition that stood out to me—the one God seemed to "put a bell on," as one of my best friends likes to say—is this:

Calling: *The work that a person does or should be doing.*

Another entry stated it this way:

Calling: *A vocation or profession.*

Some of the variations of the definition included "a strong desire" to do a work or a feeling of being "divinely led" into a work. Regardless, I couldn't miss the flag-waving common ingredient: they were all about *work.*

To say it simply, the dictionary definition of a *calling* is all about a J-O-B.

HOW ABOUT *PURPOSE*, MR. WEBSTER?

I sat for a while thinking about how anti-climactic—how utterly unromantic, how un-epic—this definition of *calling* was, and then I got another idea: *Look up the word* purpose.

Right away I knew this prompting must be straight from the Holy Spirit, because *purpose* wasn't the word I'd been obsessing over all these years. I'd never really given much thought to the idea at all. My special *calling* is what I'd been looking for, remember? Besides, weren't *purpose* and *calling* pretty much the same thing?

Look it up.

So I did. I went to the ever-faithful Dictionary.com, typed in the word, and this is what it said:

Purpose: *The reason for which something exists
or is done, made, or used.*

Let's take a look at those two definitions side-by-side and slightly condensed:

Calling: *The work that a person does.*

Purpose: *The reason for which something exists.*

I don't know about you, but I notice one thing right away: The two key words do not mean the same thing. Not the same thing at all.

LESSONS FROM THE VACUUM

I sat there a while, thinking about my new linguistic discovery. *What are You trying to show me, God? I don't really get it.*

I can just imagine the heavenly host having a good laugh sometimes at how slow I can be. I'm thankful that when I'm not really on my game, God does what He did in biblical times: He uses images that common folks (like me) can understand and apply to our lives.

For me, it is often domestic tools that "speak."

If you don't mind, I'd like to share a bit of our conversation with you.

Think of a vacuum, said the strong, gentle voice in my head. *What is the purpose of a vacuum? What's the reason it exists?*

Why, to suck up dirt, I answered with the confidence of one with a wealth of domestic knowledge.

Yes, to suck up dirt, the Almighty confirmed. *Now, I want you to imagine a king purchasing a vacuum and bringing it to his palace. If that vacuum had feelings, you can imagine how thrilled it would be to get this assignment—to be brought to such an amazing place to suck up dirt.*

Yeah, I guess that would be pretty great for a vacuum, I agreed.

Now, continued the Lord, *imagine that a different vacuum was bought by the owner of a little old shack to suck up dirt there. How do you think that vacuum would feel?*

Disappointed . . . really bummed, I said.

But, He continued, *what if the palace vacuum was placed in a closet and never brought out to suck dirt? And what if the shack vacuum sucked up tons of dirt every day? Which vacuum do you think would be more satisfied? Which would you say is living the more fulfilling life?*

Well, if you put it that way, I replied, *the shack vacuum is definitely living the better life.*

Exactly! Because the shack vacuum is fulfilling the reason for which it exists. It is sucking up dirt. It doesn't matter where. Although the palace vacuum has what might seem to be a more exciting assignment, it's not getting to do what it was made to do, and thus is not in a better position at all.

I thought I was beginning to see where this was going, but then God threw a curveball. *Now suppose that, like the shack vacuum, the palace vacuum gets to suck up dirt all day long. Which vacuum has the better life now?*

It felt like a trick question, but I knew my answer right away: *The palace vacuum, of course. A palace versus a shack? Come on. No brainer.*

There was no hiding the bias behind my answer. It was right there in plain sight, exactly where God wanted it.

IT ALL DEPENDS

As the Lord continued to walk me through the lesson step by step, I saw that it all comes down to understanding the roles and desires of the main characters in the analogy: each vacuum; and the one who paid for it, its owner.

The vacuum can be taken to a shack or a palace or anywhere else in the world to suck up dirt. That is entirely up to its owner. The one who bought the vacuum decides where it does its thing. The vacuum doesn't have to worry about it; it just has to be a vacuum. Its purpose is independent of its calling. And what pleases the owner—the main thing the one who paid for the vacuum desires—is that the vacuum faithfully suck up dirt, anywhere, anytime. *Where* it does its work isn't the primary concern. The owner simply wants the vacuum to fulfill the reason for which it exists.

The most important concern to both the owner and the vacuum is that the vacuum fulfill its *purpose*. The secondary concern is the specific way or location in which the assignment is carried out. Or, in other words . . . its *calling*.

REASON VS. WORK

By now you might be making the connection: *we* are the vacuum. Of course, I don't mean literally. But in the analogy, the vacuum is us. It's you and me. And the One who paid for us is our Divine Designer. He paid a premium price, giving up His own life. We are His, created for a purpose.

Like the vacuum, we have a *reason* for which we exist. We also have *work* to do; we have callings.

In all of this, I have come to see a crazy truth firsthand: our lives can take two entirely different paths depending on which concern we put first in our hearts as the determiner of significance in our daily lives. If, like the vacuum, we're intent on fulfilling the purpose we've been given, we can feel a sense of deep fulfillment every single day, wherever we are. Why? Because purpose never changes. It's not dependent on any circumstance or on other people; we live out our purpose by simply operating as who we are, as best we can.

If we primarily concern ourselves with our calling, however, we can expect days that end in emptiness. Why? Because callings come and go and change. Like a box of chocolates, you never know what you're gonna get; they come in all different sizes and shapes. Does it make sense to tie our daily measure of success to something that can change at any moment as God determines?

Living with a truly purpose-focused life rather than a calling-focused life changes everything. Because it doesn't matter where we are or what title we have or what vocation we embark on. We can be fully engaged in fulfilling our purpose anywhere, at any time, and in all places. We can put our heads on the pillow every single night, knowing we truly and fully *lived it.*

SO, WHAT IS IT?

Now you're probably wondering, *Well, what is it then? What's my purpose? Why do I exist?*

I'm definitely going to get to the answer, but I'd like to briefly point out something sort of neat here: Every single human on earth asks this question. It's a question that actually unites us. We're all wondering, all searching for the answer.

Still, we don't always come to the same conclusion, do we? There are many different beliefs about the purpose of human life circulating out there, and this could pose quite a confusing problem if it weren't for one important fact: there can only be one truth. No matter how many beliefs are out there, only one will line up with reality. And that's the one we want, right?

Which is why we want to go straight to the One who created all things with a grand plan in mind.

Let's take a look at what He says about our *true* purpose in His Word, the Bible.

- *Now all has been heard; here is the conclusion of the matter: Fear God and keep his commandments, for this is the duty of all mankind.* (Ecclesiastes 12:13)
- *Everyone who is called by my name, whom I created for my glory; whom I formed and made.* (Isaiah 43:7)

- *Now this is eternal life, that they may know you, the only true God, and Jesus Christ, whom you have sent.* (John 17:3)
- *[Jesus said:] I have brought you glory on the earth by finishing the work you gave me to do.* (John 17:4)
- *In Christ we have also obtained an inheritance, having been destined according to the purpose of him who accomplishes all things according to his counsel and will, so that we, who were the first to set our hope on Christ, might live for the praise of his glory.* (Ephesians 1:11-12 NRSV)
- *Whether you eat or drink or whatever you do, do it all for the glory of God.* (1 Corinthians 10:31)
- *If anyone speaks, let him speak as the oracles of God. If anyone ministers, let him do it as with the ability which God supplies, that in all things God may be glorified through Jesus Christ, to whom belong the glory and the dominion forever and ever. Amen.* (1 Peter 4:11 NKJV)

The Westminster Shorter Catechism states it ever so clearly in question-and-answer form:

> *Q: What is the chief end of man?*
> *A: Man's chief end is to glorify God, and to enjoy Him forever.*

The reason for which we exist is, in its simplest form, to glorify God.

What does this mean? It means "to give praise and honor." It also means "to magnify," making the object of our praise bigger or easier to see.

We are here to magnify God. To make Him bigger—so that a hurting and dying world can more easily see . . . *Him.*

You might be thinking, *Well, that doesn't sound like much fun.*

I get it. There was a time when I felt the same way: *What's in it for ME? What's going to happen to MY life, God, if all I'm doing is trying to make YOU famous?*

I think James 4:10 says it best: "Humble yourselves before the Lord, and He will lift you up."

To humble ourselves simply means to live our lives being exactly who we were created to be—nothing more and nothing less. Which sounds a lot like living a life of purpose, don't you think? When I live in such a way that I fulfill the reason for which I exist, exactly as God intended, the Lord will lift me up. He will lift my head and my heart so that I have joy.

If we are all about *Him,* we are guaranteed, He will be all about *us.*

But isn't it kind of conceited of God to create us to be all about making Him famous?

No. Not at all. Why? Because He knows that He is the only one who can satisfy all our needs. He is the only one who loves us unconditionally, who always and solely has our best in mind. *That* isn't called conceit; it's called *love.*

God wants us to glorify Him—to make Him easier to see—so that our friends and family (the people He has put in our lives to love) will find the Way, the Truth, and the Life and enjoy Him forever too. The best thing we can do for ourselves, and for anyone we care about, is to give ourselves completely and entirely to the purpose of knowing Him and making Him known.

HOW DID I MISS IT?

Ever since God gave me the vacuum analogy, I see its message everywhere. I see it in so many of the books I read, that I have no idea how I missed it for so many years other than, as I mentioned before, I was distracted.

I love it when God confirms what He's telling us through the words of others, especially when those "others" are older and wiser. I'd like to end this chapter by sharing some perspective from a few of my favorite theologians.

- From J.P. Moreland:

The purpose of life is to bring honor to God, to know, love and obey Him, to become like Him, and to live for His purpose in this world as I prepare to live in the next one.[1]

- From William Lane Craig:

The chief purpose of life is not happiness, but the knowledge of God. We are not God's pets, and the goal of human life is not happiness per se, but the knowledge of God—which in the end will bring true and everlasting human fulfillment. God's ultimate goal for humanity is our knowledge of him—which alone can bring eternal happiness.[2]

- From Ravi Zacharias:

Here is life's essential purpose—to worship God in spirit and in truth (see John 4:24). All other purposes are meant to be secondary.[3]

When we live to glorify God—when we keep the main thing ever before us—our burden truly is light, just as Jesus promised it would be.

I can make God easier to see. I can totally do that! I exhibit His love when I extend love. I show His mercy when I offer mercy. I put His peace, joy, and power on display when I tap into all of that for myself. When I receive His great love for me. When I walk in the grace He lavishes on me.

If I open my heart to accept all that He longs to give me, I can't help but live as a walking billboard for the King of kings. I can help my children see Him more clearly. I can help my coworkers . . . my friends . . . the guy who works in the grocery deli . . . to see God more clearly. Any day. Anywhere.

I feel like I've lost the proverbial weight off my shoulders, and I want that for you. My life has drastically changed for the better since I started living like a vacuum cleaner. Yours can change too. As long as we remember to live this way, happy to fulfill our purpose, we can avoid the pain and pitfalls of constantly looking and longing for a special calling. We will take a closer peek at these hazards in the next few chapters.

HOW ABOUT YOU?

1) In your own words, state the reason for which you exist according to the Scriptures:

2) What is most likely to keep you from living your purpose every day?

3) How would your life change if you began to live with a purpose focus rather than a calling focus?

4) Andrew Murray wrote:

The one purpose for which God gave life to creatures was that in them He might prove and show forth His wisdom, power, and goodness, in His being each moment their life and happiness, and in pouring out to them, according to their capacity, the riches of his goodness and power. And just as this is the very place and nature of God, to be unceasingly the supplier of everything the creature needs, so the very place and nature of the creature is nothing but this: to wait on God and receive from Him what He alone can give, what He delights to give.[4]

    a) According to this quote, what is the place and nature of God?

    b) What is the place and nature of the creature (you and me)?

POINTS ON PURPOSE:

» Purpose and calling are not the same. It's so important to differentiate between these two. Purpose is the reason we exist. Calling is the work we do.

» We have purpose independent of any of our specific callings. And every human being has the same *primary* purpose: to be God-glorifiers and God-magnifiers.

CHAPTER THREE

WHY THEM?

I want to begin this chapter with an important point. There is nothing wrong whatsoever with asking God for specific, clear directions, wanting to go where He leads and answer when He calls. It only becomes a problem when we *obsess* about it. When we feel we *must* have clear directions—we *must* have a special calling—or else something isn't quite right. As if life isn't fully meaningful yet, and it won't be until we find it.

Think Gollum in *The Lord of the Rings*. That poor, crazed creature was once the peaceful hobbit Sméagol, enjoying life and friends and simplicity. Until that fateful fishing trip with a buddy, the one where "The Precious" is first glimpsed—the golden ring to rule all rings. Then it's on! The obsessive need for the ring. Nothing else matters, not even the life of Sméagol's friend. And as the obsession grows over the years, the ring's all-consuming allure even trumps Gollum's self-care. So long, pearly whites and curly locks. And when the ring is lost to Frodo, Gollum cannot stop craving it. He is willing to do anything, including biting off Frodo's finger, to get that dang ring back and be able to caress it once more. But once he has his Precious again, he falls into a boiling pit of lava and dies.

Now *that's* obsessed! And though we may not go so far as to lose hair and teeth over it, we do lose other things like time, peace, and joy. That's when it's a problem. Because not only have we been duped into idol worship, but we expect God to meet us on our terms. *I want my Precious—I mean, my special calling—and I want it now!* Then our need for clear direction—for some divine directive delivered by heaven itself—becomes the object of our desire. *Gotta have it. Gotta have it now.* And *Where? When? Why?* and *How?* become the great questions of our hearts, while the question of *Who?* is promptly put on the back burner.

Much of the time we don't even realize we've back-burnered God. Our hearts are deceptive, tricking us into thinking all we want is His best. *I LOVE God! He is my all.*

Is He really though?

RELATIONSHIPS INVENTORY

Sometimes the only way to find out where God stands in our hearts is to take an honest look at how we're relating to the people in our lives. Our horizontal relationships reflect the health of our vertical one. We cannot be truly at peace with God if we don't have peace with man. After all, God made man, and God loves man.

When I say that we must be at peace with man, I don't mean we never have conflict with others. What I really mean is that we're at peace with humanity's role, humanity's brokenness, and humanity's destiny. We understand that everyone's banged up, every heart has cracks in it, and everyone is a work in progress. Not one of us has arrived; everyone has their baggage.

One of the pitfalls of constantly aching for a special calling is that we lose sight of our common ground. Forgetting that we're all in this together, we enter into a competition with just about everyone, especially other Christians. Apologist and author Ravi Zacharias uses the notables among us to make the point: "The lifestyles of the rich and famous are half-truths. Yes, they live in grander houses, but inside they breathe the same sorrows and have the same longings. Despite the gold, the residents suffer from the same decay of the body, the same longings of the heart, and the same agonies of the soul as everyone else. . . . If disappointment were a thief, it would be no respecter of persons."[1]

THE DISTRACTION OF COMPARISON

I don't think we really want to do the comparison thing. Even more, I think we hate to do it because it makes us miserable. Yet we just can't seem to help it sometimes. We can't help but compare ourselves to others.

I'll bet men do it, but I *know* women do. From the moment we enter a room, we're instantly scanning. It reminds me of Arnold Schwarzenegger's most famous role, the Terminator. The cyborg machine-man can walk into any room and have all the stats scroll right before his eyes—a digital display of every motion, every warm body, every threat—inside his sunglasses.

That's us. We women can tell within seconds of walking into a room where we stand in the lineup. Who's the shortest. Who's the tallest. Whose legs are the longest. Whose rear end is the largest (usually mine). It doesn't take us much longer to start comparing our callings. *Wow, Sally has adopted five children from Africa. I'm barely able to tolerate my own two. And Suzy, she travels all over the country training leadership groups and counseling CEOs. I'm lucky to travel to the grocery once a week. Whoa, my life is boring!*

That's when the self-adjusting begins, the jockeying for position. We might never say a word, but what's going on between our ears is often a ten-car pileup of comparison. We either succumb to feeling inferior to those we're with, putting on a fake grin until we can get home and pop the cork for our pity party, or we swing the opposite way and pride ourselves in all the other things we do so well. *I might not have adopted five kids, but darn it, I have a master's degree.*

One of the biggest bummers about all this comparing is, it makes it nearly impossible for us to really, truly love one another. We're so busy trying to make ourselves feel better that we're blind to those around us who are hurting. We hurry our way through some conversations and avoid others altogether. We huddle up in little Christian cliques of self-protection. We miss the opportunities to be "God's love with skin on" because we're so uncomfortable in our own skin.

In truth, there's no need to compete. God's love and goodness is the same toward all of us. He doesn't run out of good gifts for His kids, and He will not overlook us.

WHAT ABOUT *ME?*

I spent a lot of years comparing myself to others and wondering when God was ever going to come through for me. When would He open the one, all-important door that would lead to my ultimate life direction? The one I could tell everyone about and plaster all over Facebook?

Although I had a measure of success in truly celebrating the achievements and opportunities afforded my friends, at some point in time I would inevitably feel the ache again. Because it never quite made any sense to me what I was doing wrong. What were my friends doing that was so much better than me? Was I really that far off the mark? *I mean, come on, God. I know how Jamie gets when she's angry. She's definitely not perfect either. Why does she get all the breaks?*

Can you imagine how ridiculous it would be for vacuum cleaners to try to one-up each other? I've been guilty though. And all the while I knew enough about the Great Commandment (the one that tells us to love God completely and our neighbor as ourselves) to know my self-focus and critical analysis of others wasn't hitting the mark. I knew it wasn't right for me to harbor even a pinch of jealousy toward those who were being blessed, even though it seemed *they* were being given what I considered the ultimate answer to *my* prayers.

The disparity between how I was acting and how I wanted to be hurt my heart. *Lord, I really want to love people the way You do. Please . . . help me.*

REMEMBERING *WHO*

I don't by any means think our search for a special calling is the only thing that sets us up for this type of comparing. Sometimes it's our desire for attention or our pursuit of possessions. But aching for some extraordinary assignment in life tripped *me* up more often than anything else.

I don't know if the ache ran so deep because I wanted all the pieces of my life's puzzle to finally fit into a nice, neat picture (I am an organization freak of sorts), or if I needed to prove I deserved to exist, or if I was simply jonesing for some adventure like a middle-aged, suburban adrenaline junkie. But I do know this: the ever-present need for a special calling overshadowed my special *identity*. I spent so much time focused on what I wasn't *doing* that I missed the joy, peace, and victory found in who I *am*. You know, that one-of-a-kind soul, crafted by God Himself? That gal.

As sons and daughters of God, we have an incredible inheritance—one that no one can take from us. We don't have to earn it, and we don't have to struggle to keep it. It's just ours. And our identity is a big part of that inheritance.

Who we are is given, not earned. Like our purpose, our identity is from God and depends completely on Him. Since God is unchanging, there is nothing that can change who we are in Him. Read that sentence ten times if you must. We could become completely paralyzed or lose all our limbs—and still our identity would be intact. Who we *are* is not based on things that change, and that's one reason it can't be based on our *callings*, which can and often do change.

Here's truth: I am not Teasi Cannon. That's my name.

I am not a mom, an author, or a teacher. That's what I do.

I am not nearly fifty years old (I just simply refuse to believe that).

I am a child of God.

"Yet to all who did receive him, to those who believed in his name, he gave the right to become children of God" (John 1:12). Also . . . *"The Spirit himself testifies with our spirit that we are God's children. Now if children, then we are heirs—heirs of God and co-heirs with Christ" (Romans 8:16-18a).*

Do you know what it means to be a joint-heir with someone? It means that you get to share the inheritance. And the Bible tells us that we are joint-heirs with Christ! So whatever Christ has right now is ours too. Including His mind. Take a look at 1 Corinthians 2:12-16:

> *What we have received is not the spirit of the world, but the Spirit who is from God, so that we may understand what God has freely given us. This is what we speak, not in words taught us by human wisdom but in words taught by the Spirit, explaining spiritual realities with Spirit-taught words. The person without*

*the Spirit does not accept the things that come from the Spirit
of God but considers them foolishness, and cannot understand
them because they are discerned only through the Spirit. The person with the Spirit makes judgments about all things, but such
a person is not subject to merely human judgments, for, "Who
has known the mind of the Lord so as to instruct him?" But we
have the mind of Christ.*

I'm no master theologian, but when I read that we have the
mind of Christ, what I'm thinking is, we have access to the mind
of Christ! And if we have access to the mind of Christ, then we
have the right to tap into all we can of what He knows, what He
feels, what He desires, and what He sees. *Including what He sees
when He looks at you and me.*

If we can find ourselves in the mind of Christ, who loves us
with an everlasting love, why in the world would we want to find
ourselves in anything else?

Why would we seek to find ourselves, our worth, our value in
the dreaded digital display of the white square that sits on the
bathroom floor? Why would we seek to find ourselves in the cur-
rent balance on our bank statement? Or in the number of letters
after our name, or in the ever-changing description of our calling?

We are not nameless and faceless in God's eyes. He knows us
by name. He knows the number of hairs on our heads. And He's
weaving every thread of our lives into a beautiful tapestry. Even the
threads that aren't our favorite color. We are who Jesus says we are.

Read these out loud:

1) I am Christ's friend. (John 15:15)

2) I belong. (1 Corinthians 6:19)

3) I am the salt and light of the world. (Matthew 5:13)

4) I am a minister of reconciliation for God. (2 Corinthians 5:18)

5) Jesus is not ashamed of me. (Hebrews 2:11)

6) I am forgiven and clean. (1 John 1:9)

7) Nothing, not even my distractions, can separate me from God's love. (Romans 8:39)

I love that none of these biblical descriptors ends with the phrase: *as soon as you find your special calling.* Each of these truths (plus so many more) apply right now. To you, to me, to all of us in equal measure. Which means there's really no reason for comparing and competing. There are no orphans in God's family. No almost-sons or almost-daughters. No "most popular." No celebrities. No American idols or Miss Americas. God's mind doesn't think in those terms. He has only beloved, wanted, well-provided-for children.

THE GRASS IS NOT GREENER

Another mindset that works against us is: "I need my special calling before I can finally make a grand entrance into the work of God's kingdom." For starters, our definition of *special* is most likely not the same as God's (more about this in later chapters). Additionally, not only does waiting for that "spotlight moment" make us more keenly aware of all the fulfilled callings around us, but we might even find ourselves wishing we could have someone else's calling. We see the worship band and wish we could be worship leaders too. We meet the resident missionaries when they're home on furlough and long to move far, far away in service to the Lord. We envy the brilliant blogs of the mom-trepreneur who's got half a million readers hanging on every insightful word she posts. We imagine what it's like to be the sold-out-for-Jesus stockbroker who keeps bringing in souls while he rakes in the cash. And sometimes we go out of our way to mirror what they've done.

How did "the favored ones" get where they are today? we ask. With answers in hand, we might change our looks or our lingo; change the products we buy; change how we eat, what we post online, where we live or go to church or work, or even who we hang out with, hoping that maybe, if we look and act more like the people who have found their special calling, it will bring us a step closer to finding our own. Or sometimes we try to force someone else's calling to fit us, like the desperate stepsisters attempting to cram their big, ugly feet into Cinderella's dainty shoe. We work so hard at singing, or writing, or marketing a new business or ministry, uncomfortably contorting ourselves into a role that is obviously—sometimes painfully—not the one for us. Only it doesn't work, does it?

And here's a question: Who is going to be *me*, who is going to be *you*, while we are trying to be someone else?

No one. We're leaving our own post empty—the one God specifically assigned to us—while we long for someone else's. The people in our lives who need *us* are only getting part of us, because we're not fully living in the moment. We've become horizon watchers, missing the flowers at our feet.

While there is nothing wrong with admiring someone for their character and accomplishments, trying to actually *be* them is an unhealthy thirst that can never be quenched. Not everyone will win a Nobel Prize or be featured on *TIME* Magazine's "Most Influential" list, but there is always splendor to be found in what we consider ordinary.

Truth is, God wanted me to be me and you to be you. He likes us just the way we are, right where we are. And there is nothing more beautiful than living right smack in the middle of that.

Ironically, in those times when God gives us a backstage view of what it's like to walk in someone else's calling—the one we think we really want—we discover we don't like it that much after all. Maybe it's happened to you? Did you always dream of being a Bible teacher, but when you were asked to fill in for a Sunday School class, you ended up with a dry mouth and a sleepless night because you found you actually don't prefer being in front of people? Or maybe you got a chance to go on a short-term mission trip and learned that living your life minus air conditioning, with bug spray as your perfume, brought out the worst in you?

Yeah, things like that have happened to me too.

It just goes to show you: We don't really know what's best for us. Which is why it's best to just leave it to the One who designed us from scratch. Let Jesus decide where He wants us while we continue to focus on sucking up dirt. (Uh, you know what I mean.)

In his book *Recapture the Wonder,* Ravi Zacharias says it like this: "Until we see in ourselves the uniqueness of God's touch, we will always want to be someone else and will live under the illusion that being someone else would be better. History is full of examples of God using the most unlikely people for His extraordinary purposes."[2]

I'd rather be one of the "unlikely people" and be completely present for those whom God has placed in my life. I truly believe that the life fully lived is the life lived in the now. Not the life that keeps aching for what may or may not be coming around the corner.

HOW ABOUT YOU?

1) How do you feel when someone you know gets exactly what *you've* been praying for?

2) What does your reaction tell you about the condition of your heart? How secure are you in God's love for you?

3) What difference does it make to know you have access to the mind of Christ?

4) Missionary Jim Elliot said: "Wherever you are, be all there! Live to the hilt every situation you believe to be the will of God."

  a) In what areas could you be more present in your life?

  b) What does "Live to the hilt" mean to you? Are you doing it? What needs to change in your life to get you there?

POINTS ON PURPOSE:

» A sad byproduct of the special-calling obsession is that it often puts us in competition with others, inclining us to measure ourselves against people's accomplishments, skills, and talents, and even envy what they have.

» When we're busy asking God what He wants us to do, it's easy to forget who He's made us to be. We must remember: our identity is found in the very mind of Christ, not in anything we could possibly achieve.

CHAPTER FOUR

OPPORTUNITY COST

What do you think of the following quotes?

- *To find out what one is fitted to do, and to secure an opportunity to do it, is the key to happiness.* (John Dewey)
- *The ladder of success is best climbed by stepping on the rungs of opportunity.* (Ayn Rand)
- *Success is where preparation and opportunity meet.* (Bobby Unser)

So inspiring, right? Don't you want to get out and make something of yourself? Push just a little harder and take hold of every opportunity that comes your way? Get over the fear and just go for it?

I would absolutely appreciate every one of these great statements if it weren't for one small detail: they're all based on first *having* opportunities. I guess a gal like me is plumb out of luck if she doesn't have those.

But what are opportunities anyway? What are these all-important things on which my success and happiness seemingly depend? Here's one definition: *a favorable juncture of circumstances.* And here's another: *a good chance for advancement or progress.*

So let me see if I'm getting this straight: *Our achievement of success and happiness is based on the discovery of a favorable juncture of circumstances that offer us a good chance for advancement or progress . . .*

Circumstances and a good chance. *Okayyyy.*

Well, I definitely want to achieve success. And who doesn't want happiness? So I guess I'd better get busy drumming up some favorable junctures. Better start positioning myself for advancement and progress. After all, it's been said that "opportunities are like sunrises. If you wait too long, you miss them."

OR IS IT A HOAX?

But what if it's just not true? What if all the hoopla about seizing opportunity is flat-out misleading? A big hoax camouflaged in well-intended motivational garb?

I'm going to step out on a limb here and say that a hoax is *exactly* what it's capable of being. Why do I believe this? Because I fell for it.

For me, one huge marker of success was finally being able to figure out what God had called me to do—that special (and hugely significant) task He had planned just for me—and then getting about the business of doing it. Once this was all in place, and not a moment sooner, victory and contentment could finally be mine. This is what the equation looked like:

If *finding my calling = success*

and *success = seizing opportunities*

then *finding my calling = seizing opportunities*

Opportunities become pretty important when this is your underlying formula.

Just imagine, if you will, what a life based on this equation might look like on a daily basis. Maybe you don't have to use your imagination much because you live by it already? If so, do you see how you could be setting yourself up for feelings of failure? Do you notice the makings of a trap?

Also, consider this: Opportunities aren't just lying around for us to take advantage of any ol' time we please. They aren't something we can grab out of the pantry and whip up like a batch of cookies anytime we have a hankering. No. Opportunities must *come*. They arrive and knock. It's as if they're out there somewhere, deciding who they will grace with their presence. *Woo hoo, Opportunity! I'm over here!*

If this is our scenario, all we can do is hope for, pray for, plead for, pay for opportunities. Or we can meet up with people who seem to have already had a visit from opportunity. Maybe they could help open a door for us? Give us a helping hand? Good idea! Let's try that.

Bye bye, people. Hello, contacts!

Picture the following course of events. This may or may not be taken straight out of my own life story (wink).

Your phone signals that you've received a text. You immediately see that it's . . . the one. That incredibly successful person you've been chatting with at church has finally taken you up on the coffee date you've been suggesting. This is really, really good.

Once the day of the coffee date arrives, your heart is filled to the full with anticipation. You've so enjoyed the conversations you two have had in the past, and you have no doubt today's will be the best yet. You carefully select your attire, not wanting to look too formal, but not wanting to appear apathetic. You leave just a few minutes early so as to make a good impression.

Arriving at the coffee house, you get a parking spot right in front. Must be a sign of good things to come. *You say a quick prayer, thanking God for this incredible meeting, and head in. Finding a somewhat private table, you sit waiting (maybe you left just a tad too early), and then finally . . . Ms. Success arrives. You both order a coffee, and the conversation begins.*

To be polite, you inquire about her day and how she's doing. After a few moments of listening, it's your turn. At last. It's time to explain your situation—where God has you in your life right now, what He's challenging you about, and what great things He's been teaching you. You make sure to share just enough detail to be authentic, while trying not to sound too desperate or needy. You want this person to see how mature and ready you are for what is certain to be the new season of opportunity she will propose.

An hour passes by so quickly. You can't believe you've been talking so long, but this coffee date has been such an answer to prayer, and your heart is expectant. Even though Ms. Success has to get back to work, you're certain you will be hearing from her in the very near future. This feels like such a divine appointment. Surely God is going to use her to open the all-important door you've been waiting for.

After a couple of weeks pass with no further communication, you decide to send a quick e-mail thanking Ms. Success once more for the incredible time you had with her. You're hoping this will jog her memory. Maybe she's just been so busy that she forgot about the opportunity she wanted to offer you. Your gesture will surely be seen as a blessing. She'll be shocked she has neglected to present such an important proposal.

But when the reply is a simple, "I enjoyed it as well. Have a great day!" you don't understand. Where's the open door of opportunity? Where's the long-awaited invitation to your big calling? What happened?

Well, I can tell you. What's happened is this:

- A person—one of God's children—has become a mere contact.
- What had all the makings of sweet fellowship over coffee became a networking "event."
- The precious gift of a new day has become yet another twenty-four-hour period in which God had better get a move on and open the door to your calling!

I know all of this because, like I said, it's happened to me—more times, and with more precious folks, than I like to admit.

And when none of it pans out . . . the bottom falls out. Despair and disappointment draw the shades, and we put our head on the pillow once more, aching for something that never seems to come, longing for the hole in our existence to be filled, wondering when true life—that much-touted, more-than-abundant life—will ever start.

GOAL OR DESIRE?

I believe one of the reasons we experience such devastation when situations like this don't go our way is that we've confused desires and goals. You see, a desire is something we hope will happen, but a goal is something that can certainly happen. Neil Anderson says it so well in his book *Victory over the Darkness*: "A godly goal is any specific orientation that reflects God's purpose for your life and is not dependent on people or circumstances beyond your ability or right to control."[1]

When we set a finish line for ourselves that no circumstance or person can keep us from, we've established a solid goal. It's something we can put all our effort and prayer into and fully expect its fruition. A goal is between me and God. No one on earth can ruin it but me. If someone or something else can prevent it from happening, it should not be in the *goal* category. It should be demoted to a *desire.*

Anderson adds: "A godly desire is any specific result that depends on the cooperation of other people, the success of events or favorable circumstances you have no right or ability to control."[2] Did you catch the mention of *favorable circumstances?* Reminds me of our definition of opportunities at the beginning of the chapter.

Is this telling us that opportunities should only be in our *desire* category? I believe that's exactly what it's saying. Since I can't necessarily make opportunities happen, they should not be an official goal.

Here's a little quiz:

- **When I sincerely pray for my family to be the most Christlike family at church, is this a goal or a desire?**
  - To answer the question, we need to ask ourselves: How many people or circumstances can deter this? Well, for me, the answer is: *Four people and innumerable circumstances* (my husband, three children, and real life). With so many potential obstacles, this should definitely be in my *desire* box.

How about this?

- **I really want the job promotion I've been working so hard for. Goal or desire?**
  - Again, is there anyone or anything that can prevent this from transpiring? Well, sure. The boss could choose someone else. The company could fail. Many things could hinder it. It's definitely a *desire*.

Okay, one more:

- **I set my sights on becoming the godliest, most loving friend I can be. Goal? Desire?**
  - Can anyone or anything get in the way of this? No one but me. The only person who can keep me from being a godly friend is me. This is a proper *goal*.

CALLING IS A DESIRE

Since a calling is a profession, role, or *j-o-b*, there will always be people or circumstances that can stand in its way. This isn't to say, "You'll *never* find a calling, so just quit hoping and go eat some worms." (My understanding is that each and every one of us has several callings over a lifetime.) Rather, we should not let the *desire* for an important calling dictate our sense of peace, fulfillment, or success. That's exactly what happens, though, when we treat our calling as a goal.

Think about how you feel when you finally attain something you've set your sights on. You experience such a sense of victory, such joy and satisfaction! It's the feeling we long for every day. We humans live for joy. We love the fulfillment and peace of accomplishing a goal. God made us this way.

According to Skye Jethani, "It is not our circumstances or behaviors or radical decisions that give our lives meaning and hope, but our unity with God himself."[3] Our circumstances—or *opportunities*—do not infuse our lives with significance. And so our callings simply cannot either. It's our unity, our relationship, with God that makes our lives meaningful. Period. King David knew this. In Psalm 16:11, he said, "You make known to me the path of life; you will fill me with joy in your presence, with eternal pleasures at your right hand."

Fullness of joy is ours for the taking when we make godly *goals* our aim. Godly goals will always support God's primary purpose for our lives, which is for us to know Him and make Him known. To magnify Him in our lives while basking in His delight of us.

We don't need to *hope* for this to happen. This *can* happen every day. No person or circumstance can stand in the way of you and me getting to know our heavenly Father a little more and bragging to someone else (or to the dog, if no one is around) about His goodness. I'll bet the dog would love to hear it!

SETTING THINGS STRAIGHT

When we put purpose first, everything else falls into the proper place. When we wake up each day with the goal that we will glorify God to the best of our ability in all the activities that are before us, several wonderful things happen:

- *Our desires actually begin to change.* This is what we see in Psalm 37:4: "Take delight in the LORD, and he will give you the desires of your heart." God will actually deposit desires into our hearts, and when our desires originate with Him rather than "self" or the world, we will see them come to fruition more and more. That's the icing!

- *People become precious again.* No longer will we see them as contacts or connections, hoping they will open some grand door for us. We're also much better able to hear God's cues when He's revealing the pain in someone's tone or the distant look of hopelessness in their eyes. In such situations, we just may get to show God's love! And in so doing, we will feel our own heart filled because . . . we're living our purpose.

- *Lunches and coffees aren't self-focused networking events but times of sweet fellowship, mutual edification, and good old-fashioned fun.* We can be thankful for these chances to meet new people and see new places while remaining ever on the lookout for what God is up to.
- *Each day becomes another precious twenty-four hours in which we can be what we are created to be: God-magnifiers.* And when we go to bed at night, there will be no inner critic calling us a total loser, no overwhelming feeling of failure. Just the peace of having spent one more day with a good, good Father and the satisfaction of reaching our godly goals.

And here's another sweet twist. When we put living our purpose first and make it our true goal, we will no longer need to wait on opportunity to come knocking. In fact, opportunity won't leave us alone. From the moment our feet hit the floor in the morning until we drop into bed at night, we will have many chances to get to know God through prayer and studying His Word (even more so now, thanks to Bible apps and podcasts). And we can make Him known every time we interact with people in ways that reflect His heart.

Just for fun, let's take a look at the quotes from the beginning of the chapter with our new eyes:

- *To find out what one is fitted to do, and to secure an opportunity to do it, is the key to happiness.* (John Dewey)

- *The ladder of success is best climbed by stepping on the rungs of opportunity.* (Ayn Rand)
- *Success is where preparation and opportunity meet.* (Bobby Unser)

How does it feel reading them with your primary purpose in mind? It makes me want to say, "Let's do this thing!" There's nothing—and, more importantly, no one—stopping us!

HOW ABOUT YOU?

1) Is there anyone in your life whom you see first and foremost as a contact? How would it change your relationship with that person if living your purpose became more important than solidifying a calling?

2) What was your biggest takeaway from this chapter?

3) What goals do you have today that should be demoted to your *desire* box? Why?

4) What comes to mind when you read these words from Roy and Revel Hession? "The reason for getting right should not be that we might have revival, or power, or be used of God, or have this or that blessing, but that we might have Him. Our sin has caused us to let go of His hand; a cloud has come between His lovely face and ourselves, and at all costs we want to find Him and His fellowship again."[4]

POINTS ON PURPOSE:

» When our feelings of success and fulfillment depend on having and living a special calling, we become far too reliant on opportunities. And if the "right" opportunities don't come, our desperation can grow.

» As we inflate the value of opportunities in our minds, the value of other, truly important things is diminished. People become contacts, lunches become networking opportunities, and serving becomes a platform builder. We lose out on so much. The cost is high.

CHAPTER FIVE

A DO-DO MENTALITY

Ask most people who they are, and just after offering their name, the very next response is apt to be something like, "I'm a doctor" . . . "a teacher" . . . "a baker." What's interesting about these responses is that none of them actually answers the question. Not one of them is who they *are*.

Why do we feel so drawn to define ourselves by the things we do? I personally think one of the main reasons is that we've been tricked once again. The culture we live in has convinced us that we are more valuable when we *do* really cool things. And we're really, really valuable if we are able to multitask, out-produce others, and maximize our time. In other words, according to our culture, we are worth more the busier we are. *Busyness* has become synonymous with *meaningful*.

This is another reason I believe our focus on finding a special calling is so detrimental. Because a calling is really a *doing*. And the more elusive our calling seems, the more tempted we are to do more in order to obtain it. Before we know it, we are living with a full-blown works mentality—a mindset that predisposes us toward working for approval, value, and even self-acceptance.

SAVED BY GRACE, APPROVED BY WORKS

Most of us who adhere to the core doctrines of Christianity would say without hesitation that we are saved completely by grace. We know we can't earn our salvation no matter what we do, but it seems that's where we draw the line. Everything else that comes our way must be earned.

Now, I don't know anyone who would ever come right out and admit this, and we won't hear it from most pulpits, but we obviously believe it. It's apparent in the way we live our lives, striving to be validated.

Social networking has only made it worse, in my opinion. I actually try to avoid Pinterest for this very reason. Every time I look at all the beautiful pins, I'm overwhelmed with all that I'm *not* doing. Before opening the app, I am blissfully ignorant. But once I take even the tiniest peek, it's like my eyes are opened to the dark side. I've eaten the apple from my own personal tree of the knowledge of good and evil, and . . . *gulp*. I had no idea I was supposed to be making my own laundry detergent, or building raised-bed herb gardens out of recycled milk jugs and dental floss, or making arugula salad in a jar for my kids to take to ballgames. And let's not leave out the fortitude it takes to battle the "spirit of Pinterest," that sneaky little demon that says, *You're such a loser mom. All the really cool moms are crafters.*

Exhausting!

But Pinterest is nothing compared to Facebook and Instagram. Those silly little upraised thumbs . . . that little four-letter word *L-I-K-E.* Boy, do they do some damage! These things are dangerous because they play on our God-given need for approval.

I don't think anyone would deny that we humans have emotional needs, just as we have physical needs. Mental-health professionals define a *need* as basically anything that, when it's lacking in our lives, can cause us to become sick or even die. Yes, die.

Here's the truth. We aren't ever at peace with unmet needs; what's more, we aren't supposed to be. God intended for all our emotional needs to be completely and perfectly met by Him and only Him. But . . . He doesn't always act quickly enough; we can't see Him or touch Him; His ways aren't like ours, and therefore we don't always get what we want, and surely not when we want it. So we turn away from Him, and then we start to feel empty. To avoid the emptiness, we look to counterfeit, quick-fix gods to meet our needs. We settle for lust rather than seeking unconditional love. We strive for position rather than resting in our God-given purpose. We buy bigger houses rather than living in divine provision. And we go to people for our approval rather than getting it from above.

What better place to obtain approval from people than a social network? It's so easy to assess our ratings there. All we need is to look at the number of *likes* we have, and we know. *I'm approved by only 4 today . . . I'm approved by 116! . . . I was approved by 200 just one minute after posting that picture* (faster likes double your approval rating, you know).

No matter how hard we try to deny it, that number means something to us.

I'll admit, I've tried and tried to quit looking, but I can't help taking a peek. And it never fails: the times I think I've posted the most profound statements or inspiring quotes, I get the fewest likes. Which makes me want to take down my post and try something new. It tempts me to *conform* to what people want, to what they think is cool. It tempts me to *compare* myself to the ones who seem to get all the likes. It tempts me to start doing more of what they're doing in order to be *counted* among the truly approved. User beware: it's a minefield of rejection and feelings of failure.

BETTER CALLING, MORE APPROVAL

Before we start judging the Facebook addicts of the world, let's admit that we have affirmation issues in the church too. Jesus apparently had a soft spot for the social outcasts, and He didn't mince words when He told us that many of those who are first will be last, and the last will be first. Still, we are prone to value the more public callings above all the others. The people who have a bigger platform are given celebrity status of sorts.

Think about it. When was the last time you saw a long line of people waiting their turn just to get a chance to personally thank the nursery workers after church on Sunday? Or thronging around the head greeter to share the confirming word God spoke to them during the service? Probably never, because that line is forming for the pastor or the worship leader. There's just something about that stage . . .

But it's not always bigger platforms we admire; sometimes it's greater distances traveled. For some reason, it's a *much better* special calling if one does it in Africa versus in one's own community. And at times it's a bigger number of children. Being a parent is an okay calling, but being a parent of fifteen is a fantastic calling, and even more so if at least half the children are adopted from a faraway land (double the likes)!

Please don't misunderstand. I'm not trying to belittle any of these callings AT ALL! People I adore are doing each and every one of these things. I'm just trying to level the playing field regarding all the other callings. Raise the rest of them up; don't push any down. After all, what is it that makes parenting fifteen children a grander calling than that of a single mom who is raising one child? What makes teaching a thousand adults a bigger deal than teaching ten second graders? What makes serving the poor in a foreign land more important than serving them in your own backyard? What makes singing in front of a congregation more glamorous than singing praise songs to your babies?

Nothing actually makes these callings more important, but one thing makes them *seem* more important—and that's the amount of approval they receive. Sadly, though there is no valid reason for it, we make a bigger deal out of the callings that get the most attention. And we falsely believe that our lives are somehow less if we are called to anything but. In fact, I would venture that we've been so mesmerized by the continual lure of our special calling that just about all of us feel destined for some sort of stage. Something grand. Something big. Something very in-the-spotlight. *Surely I won't be called to something small? Right, Lord?*

VISIONS OF GRANDEUR

I honestly wonder if we are doing people a grave disservice when we tell them that God has "big plans" for them. Don't we do it all the time, though, convinced that the earlier in their lives we start, the better?

Little Cindy Lou, God made YOU special. He made you with something AMAZING in mind. You are part of the next generation of KINGDOM HEROES! You and your entire VBS crew are going to be WORLD-CHANGERS some day! You are not made for the ordinary!

Wow! Cindy Lou has a lot to live up to now, doesn't she? There's a lot riding on her figuring out this big plan and doing all that world-changing.

There are a couple different roads she might take to get there.

1) Cindy might work her tail off trying to prepare for the big moment when she gets the call to jump on the world-changer bus and head to Amazingville. She will work hard to be the best little Christian girl she can be. She'll have a nice, neat checklist, and she'll hold to it. Each day she'll say her prayers (check), read her devotional (check), say *Yes, ma'am* or *Yes, sir* to all adults (check), avoid the use of curse words (check), study hard (check), graduate

with honors (check), attend every Bible study and church event she can (check), go on mission trips (check), and if her big opportunity still hasn't come, she'll begin to volunteer for everything at church (check), attend even more Bible studies (check), marry a good Christian man (check), keep her house spotless (check), diligently cut coupons and pinch pennies (check), keep herself fit (check), have a couple of beautiful babies and raise them to love Jesus (check), and, if the bus to Amazingville still hasn't come, she'll keep a smile on her face at all costs. But deep inside Cindy will start to wonder what she's done wrong. What more should she have done. And although her life will be so good, *good* isn't *amazing*. Surely this can't be what she's called to. She must have failed. She was supposed to be something *special.*

Or . . .

2) Knowing that she's not made for the ordinary, she might only tolerate school, because all this *learning* stuff is so carnal, so worldly. She will barely earn her high school diploma, but that's okay—future Kingdom Heroes don't need college! She has better things to do, like hitting the road with three friends and a guitar to raise money for her mission trip around the globe. Cindy will be footloose and fancy free, living in the moment, laughing a lot and loving animals, nature, and all things creative. She'll create a GoFundMe account for menial expenses like rent or food—things normal people get a job for. But she's meant for something special, so she doesn't need to work. Responsibilities are so . . . rigid. And commitments will tie her down. She needs to be free when the bus for Amazingville shows up.

Eventually she'll marry an artist she's met on one of her trips to Colorado, and they'll live in a van down by the river. After the first baby, she and her husband will be forced to leave their dreamy home-on-wheels and move into her parents' basement, just until their big ministry opportunity comes. But after baby number two starts school, Cindy Lou will begin to wonder why none of it seems very fun anymore. Why does she feel so tied down by menial tasks like laundry and grocery lists? This surely isn't the grand plan she was made for. After all, she's Cindy Lou! Did God forget how *special* she is?

Now, before you label me a heretic, please admit you know at least one or two people who fit the above descriptions. There are those who work themselves silly trying to earn their special calling, and those who sit around waiting for the calling to earn them. And we the Church have played a hand, no matter how unwittingly, in putting them there.

With the best intentions in mind, we're encouraging each other to bits. When we stretch the truth like we do, we're setting each other up for failure. What we often overlook, however, is that the truth doesn't need to be stretched. The truth is tremendous just as it is.

NOTHING BUT THE TRUTH

We are all special. We're special because humanity is God's special creation. Of all the breathtaking things He made, we are the only creatures fashioned in His image.

We are most definitely extraordinary. We are the only beings on earth who reason like we do, feel as deeply as we do, understand all we do, and can hope like we do. Very special indeed. Which, by the way, is why the devil hates us so much.

But is there something so mind-bogglingly special about Teasi Cannon? Am I more extraordinary than all other human beings simply because I'm me? I don't think so. And I don't need to be. When we understand the honor and privilege of being God's special creation—able to commune with Him, able to know Him, free to love Him—it's more than enough.

In his book *Imagine Heaven* (which I recommend to everyone, by the way), John Burke says it this way: "God made you for himself—not to prove your glory, but to *be* his glory. His pride and joy. His beloved son or daughter. What he wants you to do is learn to be secure in his love, in who he made you to be, and from that place of security, you can do what he created you to do. And first and foremost, this is to love those you uniquely can love."[1]

Yes, God does have *amazing* things planned for all of His kids. They're called *redemption* and *eternity*. We don't have to be punished for our sins, and we don't have to die, people! Pretty amazing, don't you think? We get to live forever with the Creator of the universe. When this body breathes its last, it won't be the last of me. *Incredible.*

But that's so far off in the future. And how do I know it's really true anyway? I'll tell you how you can know it's true. Because Jesus did exactly what He promised He would. He was crucified. I mean truly, truly dead. He wasn't "mostly dead" like the beloved Wesley in *The Princess Bride*. No, He was dead. And then He was wrapped in about seventy pounds of burial cloths, put inside a cave behind a seriously monstrous stone, and left for days.

But He didn't stay there.

He came out of that tomb and was seen by multitudes of eyewitnesses. He ate with people, talked with people, and did some amazing things like walking through walls and traveling at the speed of thought. He did all of this to show us what to expect. To show us that the grave has been defeated. That death has lost its sting. And there is so much evidence for this historical event, it has turned people like J. Warner Wallace, a former atheist and CSI detective, into a full-time minister and defender of the risen Lord.

One day, Warner got the idea he would treat the death of Christ like a cold case: he would follow the leads and the evidence, just the way he would with any other crime, and let the facts speak for themselves. And they did! Don't take my word for it. Get his book, *Cold-Case Christianity*.[2]

Because of Christ's heroism, we all have the chance to follow in His footsteps and be kingdom heroes in every one of our callings. When someone at work is feeling hopeless and lonely, our smile and friendly *hello* might save the day. When our friend is at her wit's end, we can offer to keep her kids and save the day. When our daughter thinks she's fat and ugly, we can remind her that her value is not found in this world's eyes but in the eyes of Christ—and save the day. Heroes. All around.

What about world-changers? Can we be this? Yes. We can, and we are meant to. We are meant to impact the world by being salt and light. True change—lasting change—takes time and diligence. I don't believe there are really many big world changes. Just a lot of little ones that begin to add up. Still, everywhere we go, there is change because we have the Change-Agent living inside us. The World-Changer is our Lord, and when we follow Him, we transform the world too. One life, one situation, one circumstance at a time.

What about the ordinary? Are we made to soar above it? I don't necessarily think so. But I also don't think there's anything ordinary when you're a follower of an *extra*-ordinary Savior. I truly believe there is majesty in the mundane, divine in the daily. More to come on that later.

A BIG RELIEF

When we get honest about what's true and what's hype, we are bound to feel relief. I'm sure we can all agree, it's just plain exhausting trying to be super-special every day—it's like constantly living on the set of a television show . . . pretending. How refreshing to stop climbing that endless ladder to the top. No more striving and jostling; no more positioning ourselves to be noticed in order to prove how great we are (to others or to ourselves). What an incredible thing to feel like it's all . . . enough. To enjoy what *is* rather than trampling on today in order to get to tomorrow. And once we lay hold of this new reality, our shining-star moments will be those moments in which *God* shines. Our new "I've made it to the top" will be doing our best to serve God right where we are.

Doing our best to serve God right where we are? Doesn't that mean we still have to work at it?

Yes. And no. Work is still involved. We can't expect to sit on the couch eating Oreos all day. But here's the difference: We don't *have* to work. We *get* to work.

When we are secure in God's great love for us, thankful to be a God-magnifier, it comes with a real excitement about using our best efforts to glorify Him. The work I do now is all about being the best God-magnifier I can be, wherever I am. And it's simply amazing.

HOW ABOUT YOU?

1) Which callings have you considered to be better or bigger than others? Be honest.

2) Do you feel disappointed or relieved after reading this chapter? Why do you think that is?

3) Ravi Zacharias has written: "Sadly, the drive to become number one is often the very thing that ultimately destroys

a person. It simply cannot deliver the fulfillment we seek."
What are your thoughts?[3]

4) What makes daily life with Jesus truly amazing (rather than
hyped-up amazing)?

POINTS ON PURPOSE:

» It's tempting to believe that the bigger the platform, the
grander the risk . . . or the more exotic the location, the
more special the calling. And the more special the calling,
the more affirmation we will receive. But our needs for affirmation can only be met in God and His great love for us.

» When we understand the honor and privilege of being
God's special creation—able to commune with Him, able
to know Him, free to love Him—it's more than enough.
We are special because we are His treasure, not because of
what we do.

CHAPTER SIX

IS *CALLING* IN THE BIBLE?

How did we get here? What is it that has us thinking something big is destined to happen in our lives, and the ordinary is something to avoid at all costs? Does God tell us this?

To be sure, there are many biblical accounts of people who were called to some pretty important tasks. I think we can all agree that building a humongous boat in order to save the human race despite ridicule and isolation is a pretty significant calling. And leaving everything you've ever known at seventy-five years old, just out of the blue, in order to follow God to a place you've never been and become the father of a nation that doesn't yet exist . . . yeah, that's big. Or being used as God's mouthpiece against the false gods of the Egyptian super-nation and ultimately negotiating a world-altering, release-of-captives deal. Epic for sure.

And yes, there are plenty of other accounts of people God asked to do larger-than-life things: Joshua, Rahab, David, Solomon,

Daniel, Esther, Elijah, Jeremiah . . . to name just a few from the Old Testament. And then there are our New Testament heroes: Mary and Joseph, John the Baptist, Peter, John, Luke, Paul, and the like. These are the folks of flannelgraph fame. True heroes of our faith who I personally can't wait to meet in heaven one day. There are not enough thank you's to even remotely compensate for their deposit and example to us.

Reading about their lives in the Bible, we do see examples of *calling*. But what we don't see are reports of any angst prior to the call. We don't read of Noah praying and fasting, hoping for God to show Him the special plan crafted just for his life. We don't see Abraham weeping in his tent, wondering when God will ever unveil the mighty calling with his name on it. We don't read any teenage journals from David begging God to call him out of the ordinary sheep fields into greatness. We don't see Mary studying up on how to become a woman of destiny and offering to God her grand spiritual résumé.

From all I can tell, there's simply no biblical precedent for the "beforehand anxiety" that has become so common in the Western church today. No desperation. No pushing or positioning in order to be recognized. No frantic platform building, nor any coming to the altar in desperate hopes of a prophetic word. Nope. Just normal people living normal lives, honoring God in their hearts.

And then it came: God's call to move, to act, to work, to serve. And those men and women obeyed—most of them after strong protests and in spite of feeling completely inadequate.

NOT ABOUT THEM

Apparently, our spiritual forerunners were just normal folks doing whatever was in front of them to do. When they were called by God to go and accomplish something specific, they knew Who it was all about. They were not in it for themselves. The increase they were after was the increase of the knowledge of God in all the nations, or the increase of God's righteousness in a sinful world. Definitely not the increase of their own public platform, or an increase of prosperity and exciting opportunities. Most of them knew they weren't headed down easy street, and many lost their lives for answering the call.

God used these people to further His cause, a plan He's had since before the beginning of time. To fill the earth with His glory— to bring all the earth to Himself—was supposed to be Adam's job, then Noah's, then the Israelites', now ours. Every God-initiated calling is about that. Always has been and always will be.

I honestly believe we all want that. True Christ followers want God's glory to fill the earth. And if we could just keep it at that, we'd be golden. But we don't. We subconsciously add on our own aspirations, maybe our longing for excitement, convinced that some callings will offer us more of *the good stuff* than others. Even though God never included a "Best Callings" chart in the Bible, we've tacked it on as a personal Appendix A, and consequently, we've gone off track. But we can find our way back.

In God's economy, all the things He calls His children to are meant to bring about the same glorious end: the spread of His name and love over the earth. If the ultimate end of all callings is to declare the glory of a divine God, doesn't it seem logical to say that all God-given callings are divine?

"Every calling that honors God's purpose for life in general is a sacred call," says Ravi Zacharias.[1] I love that line because it reminds us of what matters most. I don't think we would ever see our biblical heroes measuring their callings against one another's because the end was primary in their hearts, not the means. The extent and duration of their callings varied, but the goal was always the same: make God famous.

It is the same reason for which God calls us.

The God who made the world and everything in it, being Lord of heaven and earth, does not live in temples made by man, nor is he served by human hands, as though he needed anything, since he himself gives to all mankind life and breath and everything. And he made from one man every nation of mankind to live on all the face of the earth, having determined allotted periods and the boundaries of their dwelling place, [Why?] that they should seek God, and perhaps feel their way toward him and find him. Yet he is actually not far from each one of us, for "In him we live and move and have our being." (Acts 17:24-28a ESV)

BUT WHAT ABOUT *MY* FUTURE AND HOPE?

I understand I'm here for God, but doesn't the Bible tell us that God has a future and a hope just for me? Something adventurous planned?

Yes, God has plans for you because He loves you. In fact, His plans for you are more glorious than anything you could imagine, and that's not just a bumper sticker or a refrigerator magnet.

God says it this way through the apostle Paul in 1 Corinthians 2:9: "As it is written, 'No eye has seen, nor ear heard, nor the heart of man imagined, what God has prepared for those who love him.'"

There is no doubt God intends to give good gifts to each of His children. No need to think we have to go without simply because we decide to put the desire for a special calling in its proper place. Jesus tells us in chapter 11 of Luke's Gospel: "What father among you, if his son asks for a fish, will instead of a fish give him a serpent; or if he asks for an egg, will give him a scorpion? If you then, who are evil, know how to give good gifts to your children, how much more will the heavenly Father give the Holy Spirit to those who ask him!" (vv. 11–13 ESV).

Do you see the parallel structure in those verses? Jesus is saying this: If evil, goofball people like us understand how to give good gifts to our children, you can guarantee that our heavenly Father, who is perfect in every way and who owns all of heaven and earth, will give good gifts to His kids. But Jesus goes a little farther and tells us what the good gift actually is . . . and it's not a special calling.

The good gift is the Holy Spirit, the One whose fruit is love, joy, peace, patience, kindness, goodness, gentleness, and self-control. If we take a close look at everything we've ever asked God for, don't we in all truthfulness find the true fulfillment right there in Him? Isn't the answer to everything we long for found in the fruit of the Holy Spirit? I think so. And in light of that, there is no better gift.

God's good plan for His people is salvation. Salvation now and forever. Salvation from the penalty of our sin, and salvation from everything that keeps us bound and broken. He has healing, freedom, and wholeness in mind for us.

Take a look at what Jesus declares about Himself in Luke 4:17-21:

> *And the scroll of the prophet Isaiah was given to him. He unrolled the scroll and found the place where it was written, "The Spirit of the Lord is upon me, because he has anointed me to proclaim good news to the poor. He has sent me to proclaim liberty to the captives and recovering of sight to the blind, to set at liberty those who are oppressed, to proclaim the year of the Lord's favor." And he rolled up the scroll and gave it back to the attendant and sat down. And the eyes of all in the synagogue were fixed on him. And he began to say to them, "Today this Scripture has been fulfilled in your hearing."*

Bam! That must have been the ultimate, drop-the-mic moment. Can't you just see the crowd's faces? Jesus was claiming to be the long-awaited Messiah who would bring the kingdom of God to earth by preaching the gospel to the poor, healing the brokenhearted, proclaiming liberty to captives, giving sight to the blind, and liberating the oppressed. I don't know about you, but I'll take freedom from oppression and healing for my brokenness all day long! Those are pretty incredible gifts.

If we could somehow put our longing for a special calling under a microscope, I wonder what we'd find at its molecular level? What would we see underneath all the layers? Could it be that what's actually there is a need for joy? Or maybe a need for peace or patience or self-control? I wonder if we'd see that it's not a big plan we are aching for, but simply more of Him—the Comforter, the Holy Spirit?

And maybe we'd start asking for what—or Who—we really need.

WHAT WE ARE ALL CALLED TO

It's completely natural for us to have a desire to do things. God gave Adam tasks as soon as he was created: he was assigned the job of naming all the animals and tending a garden. It's in our DNA to *do*. Even after we've rearranged our priorities by putting our purpose before our calling, we will have stuff to keep us busy. And we will always want to be poised and ready for God to call us to anything at any time.

Listening for God's call is good. Obsessing? Not good. And as we open ourselves to hearing *all* the things He's calling us to rather than just the *big* things, we'll find that what He has in mind is always wonderful.

What are we called to? This is far from an exhaustive search, but just for fun, let's look at a few things we find in God's Word:

You, my brothers and sisters, were called to be free. But do not use your freedom to indulge the flesh; rather, serve one another humbly in love. For the entire law is fulfilled in keeping this one command: "Love your neighbor as yourself." (Galatians 5:13-14)

We are called to freedom. In this letter, Paul is speaking against legalism and a religious spirit. So many of the believers in Galatia were in bondage to works—trying to earn their position with

God—when amazing grace was on offer. That same grace and freedom from religious to-do lists is on offer to us.

Do you feel like you *must* read your devotional or Bible app every day? Or pray for twenty minutes each morning? If so, you're not answering your call to freedom. I'm not suggesting we should abandon our quiet time by any means, but let's remove the obligation and make it a celebration. A celebration of our intimacy with a good God who loves us and wants us. A celebration of the hope that lives within us. Let's do it because we *want* to. Anything else ends up being bondage.

> *But you are a chosen people, a royal priesthood, a holy nation, God's special possession, that you may declare the praises of him who called you out of darkness into his wonderful light.*
> (1 Peter 2:9)

We are called out of darkness. What does the word "darkness" represent to you? Depression? Deception? Anger, anxiety, or fear? No matter what it represents, God has called you out of it. And into His marvelous light.

We are living in dark times for sure. Yet as has been true for believers in all eras, we've been called out of that darkness to live lives that are different. Set apart from the world, but still present.

In order to bring light to an ever-darkening world, we must first have the Light shine on us. We are like glow-in-the-dark bracelets. Just as those fun little arcade treasures won't get their glow on until they've had full exposure to a light source, we can't expect to brighten our world until we've been fully exposed to the Light.

What does this mean? I think it means we need to chill out and let God love us. We need to sit in His presence more, without saying so much, and let Him wrap us up in His arms. This isn't easy for us to do because we're so ready to go, go, go. But the only way out of darkness is into the light. We turn on God's light when we turn off our phones, our computers, and all the other noise. Even if it's only for a few minutes each day, we are called into the light. Are we answering that call?

> *There is one body and one Spirit, just as you were called to one hope when you were called; one Lord, one faith, one baptism, one God and Father of all, who is over all and through all and in all.* (Ephesians 4:4-6)

We are called to one hope. In what have we put our hope? There are so many places we put our hope, sometimes without even realizing it. We put our hope in a diet. In a retirement plan. In our children becoming strong believers. In our health insurance. In our pastors or church programs. In our national leaders. But none of these is the one hope to which we are called. Our one hope is meant to be Jesus, the One for whom, by whom, and to whom all things exist.

It's a beautiful thing when our hope becomes simply Him. When we desire to know Him more, to see Him at work, and to hear His voice.

When the reward is His face and not His hand at work in our lives, things change. We long to hear Him no matter what He says, just for the sound of that beautiful voice. When God alone is our one true hope, then we've a hope that won't be dashed, demoted, or overanalyzed. Remember, He is a rewarder of those who diligently seek Him.

If He is not our one hope, He loves us enough to give us permission to boldly approach His throne of grace. There we can get honest with Him and ask Him to help us remove anything that is seated in His rightful place within our hearts. If we are willing to answer our call to one hope, the Lord will be faithful to meet us where we are and continue the work He has begun.

To the church of God that is in Corinth, to those sanctified in Christ Jesus, called to be saints together with all those who in every place call upon the name of our Lord Jesus Christ, both their Lord and ours. (1 Corinthians 1:2 NKJV)

We are called to be saints. In the New Testament, believers in Jesus are referred to as saints. Sometimes we'll hear Christians say, "I'm a sinner saved by grace." And while that's partly true, the part that's wrong is dangerously wrong. Yes, we are saved by grace. But once saved, we are no longer identified as sinners. We are saints (redeemed people) who sometimes sin.

Why does it matter? Because the way we identify ourselves dictates our behaviors and, in many ways, determines what we will put our thoughts and energies toward. Let's look at an example.

What do runners do? They run. If a man identifies as a runner, we can assume that he runs regularly. He most likely puts energy and thought into buying the best shoes for running, reading the best information about running, hanging with other people who run. If he identifies as a runner, he will want to be the best runner he can be. It's natural to want to be good at what we identify with.

If a woman identifies herself as a crafter, she will be all about crafting. She will probably have several boxes of craft supplies in her home, subscribe to crafting websites, attend or even teach crafting classes, and maybe have a crafting blog. She will make lots of beautiful handiworks, the more unique the better. She will hang with other crafters, etc.

So, how about a person who says, "I'm a sinner"? While you aren't likely to find this individual subscribing to *Sinner's World* magazine, you can probably predict what he or she will expect to do. Sinners sin. It's just natural.

This is why I believe we are called to be *saints* instead. Saints are followers of Christ, and when we identify as such, what do you think we will be more prone to do? Follow Him. Desire to be like Him in all we think and do. Aspire to be the best servant of Christ we can be.

Are we answering our call to be saints?

THE MOST IMPORTANT CALL OF ALL

The most important call of all is this:

You also are among those Gentiles who are called to belong to Jesus Christ. (Romans 1:6)

There it is, in black and white. We are called to belong to Christ.

In this portion of Paul's greeting to the Roman believers, we find the most essential of any calling we will ever have. It's not a call to any special profession or even a particular action. We are called to a Person, the Lord Jesus.

What does this mean? It means so many things.

It means we never need to feel like we don't belong. We are invited on a daily basis to belong to Jesus. His arms are open, calling us to come to Him, to be His.

It means we have a safe place, a home, a Protector, a Defender. We are not alone. We are not orphans.

It also means that all our Bible reading, church attendance, and prayer times are about a relationship, not a religion. We're being called to get to know Jesus—His heart, desires, commands, and promises. We can relate to Him as a person, not as some imaginary entity that is cold and distant. We can talk to Him like we talk to other loved ones. When I used to text or call my earthly brother, who died recently, I didn't start the conversation with, "Dear earthly brother . . ." Our conversations with Jesus, or even with God the Father, don't need to start so formally every time either. While we don't ever want to be irreverent, we can be familiar because we are called to a relationship.

It also means we don't belong to this world. This world is not our home, and it does not define us. The only One who has the right to define us is the One to whom we belong: Jesus. The Maker of heaven and earth. And what does He say? He says we are beloved, joint-heirs, a wonderfully made workmanship of His very own.

ANSWERING DAILY

Can you see that we are all called to some pretty amazing things every single day? When I live responding to just the few invitations we discussed in this chapter, it's enough to keep me busy until I move in to heaven. I don't think we'll ever finish answering our call to one hope, into the light, to belong to Jesus. It's an adventure that never ends.

And here's what's super-cool about all the things we *know* we're called to: answering those calls leads us to the truest contentment we can ever experience. Unlike jobs that take us far and wide, may come and go, or might never happen at all, our sure callings are steadfast, certain, and bring lasting results. And isn't that what we really long for? A calling that is pure and incorruptible? One that can't be tarnished by the cares and distractions of this world and is everlasting and immune to decay?

Lord Jesus, our true Calling, may we never settle for anything less than You.

HOW ABOUT YOU?

1) Why do you think the desire for a big calling has become so prominent in the lives of many believers?

2) What is your heart asking for right now? Is it joy? Peace? What is the ultimate answer?

3) Which of the daily things to which we are called resonates with you most? To which of those callings do you most need to respond?

4) According to Roy and Revel Hession: "We do not have to go beyond Him to something else to satisfy our needs. He is the end of all that we need, and the simple, easily accessible way to the end."[2]

 a) How is Jesus the end of all you need today?

 b) What, if anything, might be standing in the way of you accessing Him?

POINTS ON PURPOSE:

» There are many biblical characters who, we'd all agree, had pretty amazing callings. But we never see them aching for their calling, begging God to reveal His special plans for them. What we see is men and women living ordinary, faithful lives who are called with virtually no warning to further service. Most of these calls were very costly, ending in persecution and even death.

» Truth is, we are all called to eternal things. We're called to freedom, called out of darkness, called to be saints, called to one hope. And most importantly, we are called to our Savior, Jesus Christ, and His eternal kingdom. This world is not our home.

CHAPTER SEVEN

WHAT'S SO GREAT ABOUT PURPOSE?

At this point in our journey together, there may be folks who agree with the calling piece. They can see that all the stress and worry about doing something big isn't doing us any favors. But maybe they're not extremely thrilled about the primary purpose I've proposed—or rather, that God has proposed. Maybe the thought of living an entire life solely to glorify Him isn't igniting a flame of passion within.

Others of you may be totally in, excited about the idea of living life as a God-glorifier. You're ready to go.

Still others may find themselves somewhere in between.

No matter where we are on this spectrum, one thing is true: our God-given purpose is great. It's great because our God is great. One way to become excited about our purpose is to get more excited about our God. So, let's do it.

GOD IS REAL

It may seem an elementary place to start, but truly one of the greatest and most exciting things about God is that He is real. No matter what some may believe, the evidence for God's existence is simply overwhelming. And it is within this very evidence that we are able to see what an incredible purpose we have.

You may already know this, but there's an entire field of study that focuses on what is real. It's called *metaphysics*. There is another field of study that focuses on how we *know* something is real, and that is *epistemology*. Isn't that crazy? There are people who actually devote their entire lives to figuring this stuff out! Just imagine a laboratory full of PhDs wandering around, finger to chin, wondering, *Is this real? How do we know?*—and getting paid for it! I'm sure there's a lot more to it than that, but the fact that these fields of science exist has me thinking that this quest to know what is real matters quite a bit.

Right now you might feel fairly secure in your acceptance of God's existence. You're not questioning whether He is real, which is awesome. Ever since God started overwhelming me with His grace and love, I've had very few days that I doubted His existence, so I can relate. Even so, every time I look at the evidence for the reality of God, it excites me. It strengthens my faith in Him, making me all the more enthused to be called His own, and even more thrilled about my purpose.

One of the lines of evidence that continually intrigues me is seeing all the signs of intelligent design in the universe. We are made of and surrounded by patterns, finely tuned factors, and organized systems that collectively point to a genius Creator.

According to forensic principles that are used to piece together evidence in order to solve crimes, there are two main types of "cause" in our world: natural cause and intelligent cause. When we lay eyes on a breathtaking view like Crater Lake in Oregon, we pretty much assume it's there due to natural causes. We know it's a volcanic lake, and thereby can accept that it came to be as a result of past volcanic activity. But when we look at the features of a Disney waterpark, we don't think, *Wow, that must have been quite a hurricane that came through here!* No. We know someone must have designed the park. Someone drew up blueprints and made models. Things that purposeful and precise don't just happen.

How simple can something get and still qualify for having an intelligent cause? If you opened up your Scrabble game and the lettered tiles read *P-I-E*, already arranged in the box, what would you think? Accident or intelligence? Could be either. But . . . what if the tiles were neatly arranged in this order: *I LIKE PIE*. Now what would you think? Accident or smarts? Intelligence, of course. The chances of the letters just accidently arranging themselves in a sequenced sentence with all the right spacing are virtually none. No one would believe you if you claimed the message just appeared in the box naturally. Even though it's a very simple three-word sentence, we all know that a brain must be behind it.

Scientists who are involved in the SETI (Search for Extra-Terrestrial Intelligence) affirm this concept too—at least when it comes to aliens. These "SETIans" are the folks who spend their lives listening to soundwaves from outer space, hoping to hear a message. If they ever get so much as a series of patterned signals, they will assume it's from intelligence—*beep, beep, beep*—and this mystery within the cosmos will be a settled matter once and for all. Why? Because repeated patterns don't happen accidentally.

Somehow, though, many of these same scientists change the rules when they observe the obvious symmetry found in the human body or in the cycles of nature. Even more mind-boggling, they ignore the loads of detailed messaging found in one strand of human DNA.

Just to dredge up your favorite memories from high school biology, think about DNA. Do you remember that DNA strands look like a double helix—a ladder—with rungs made up of four nitrogen bases? Did you have to make a model of it out of pipe cleaners and colored beads like I did? Well, anyway, the rungs of the DNA ladder are comprised of adenine, thymine, cytosine, and guanine, and they are represented by the letters *A, T, C,* and *G*. These letters are the four-letter alphabet that "communicates" genetic messages.

When we want to relay a message using our standard alphabet, we put the letters in a specific order to form different words and phrases depending on what we want to say. Our genetic letters do the same thing. Their specific order sends a chemical message, and the message is an instruction for our bodies to do everything they do. Nothing happens without these instructions, so they have to be very specific. After all, our bodies are incredibly complex machines.

WHAT'S SO GREAT ABOUT PURPOSE?

Not only is the amount of information found in DNA specific, it's immense.

The genetic messaging found in just one single-celled amoeba is mind-blowing. Even Richard Dawkins, a professor of zoology at Oxford University who is considered one of atheism's modern heroes, admits that the message found in just the nucleus of a tiny amoeba contains more content than all thirty volumes of the *Encyclopaedia Britannica* combined, and that the entire amoeba has as much information in its DNA as a thousand complete encyclopedia sets.[1] For you younger ones who've never held an actual encyclopedia in your hands, just trust me when I tell you, they are very thick books—sort of an Internet in print.

If an explorer happened upon just a single page of only one volume of an encyclopedia, we'd undoubtedly know that an intelligent source was behind it. Even if we saw one paragraph on one page, we'd know. So it's mindboggling to me that trained scientists can be well aware of how complex and specific the genetic messages of DNA are, and still refuse to accept the idea of a divine intelligence behind it all. But a gloriously patterned *beep, beep, beep*? Now that's a different story! Suddenly ET has phoned home!

Okay, I might be enjoying a bit of sarcasm here, but do you blame me? Sometimes I think people have lost the proverbial forest for the trees. God is speaking so loudly that they can't hear Him.

We have an incredibly intelligent God who is leaving His fingerprints everywhere to be found. I urge you to research more of this for fun. (I share some websites and resources with you in the back of the book). Start with *anthropic constants.* These are all the ingredients that must exist in precise, perfect amounts for human life to survive. Things like oxygen level. Too much, and we'd all catch on fire; too little, and we'd suffocate. Gravity: too much, we would collapse in on ourselves; too little, we'd float away. Scientists are continually discovering more of these constants. There are over one hundred of these factors that have to be *just right,* as Goldilocks would say, in order to sustain human life. Incredible.

GOD IS LOVE

But our God isn't great simply because of how big and incomparably smart He is. He's also great because of how tender and personal He is. A God who defines Himself as love is one worth getting to know (see 1 John 4:8). No other being in the known world can claim that identity. This makes Him exciting to me.

Some people, though, have a hard time believing that God is loving. And it's easy to see why. All one has to do is turn on the nightly news to witness natural disasters, hate crimes, and persecution of the innocent—things that make an honest person wonder, *How can a loving God allow all of this?*

I think everyone has grappled with this question at some point. We wonder why God doesn't stop the ugliness, or even more, why He ever allowed evil to enter the scene to begin with. After all, He knows the future, so He knew it would happen. Why didn't He do something about it long ago?

These are sincere and important questions. They are so significant and hard to grapple with at times that many people refuse to bother with God. But then there are the countless, amazingly good things He has done too. Natural wonders, puppies and babies, laughter and salvation. How do we put it all together? I'm not even going to pretend to have all the answers to questions like this that have boggled minds far greater than mine. But there are things I've considered that bring a little order to the chaos and hold out hope and a measure of peace.

One of those things is this: although God is all-powerful, it doesn't mean He creates logically impossible things. For example, would God create a married bachelor? Or a circular triangle? How about a free person who is only permitted to do good things? A bound free person? Doesn't make sense, does it? So I wonder, what are the chances of any group of free human beings (no matter how large or small) only and always choosing to do good? Even when there were just two people, Adam and Eve, they couldn't stay on the straight and narrow. And they only had one bad choice in front of them. A single wrong option amid so many right ones, and they picked it! Literally.

Again, I don't have all the answers, but I do know that God decided (for reasons we may not know until eternity) to give the human race freedom. What a gift! Unfortunately, we have used that freedom in stupid and painful ways since the beginning of mankind.

I personally think one of the reasons God gave us freedom has to do with love. Although we often talk about *feeling* love,

LORD, WHERE'S *MY* CALLING?

love isn't truly a feeling; it's a choice. And there is no such thing as choice without freedom, right? Since God is love, it seems reasonable that He would want to have children who love Him, and who reflect love in return. In order to have children who love Him, God would have to give them freedom to choose. That's what He did in the Garden. The choice He set before Adam and Eve is essentially this: *I love you, and I made you. I want to provide everything for you, take care of you, and enjoy you forever. I'm giving you the freedom to accept My love, and in doing so, I'm giving you the freedom to accept Me. Will you choose Me?*

The Maker of heaven and earth made Himself an *option.* Talk about *humility!*

In order for Adam and Eve to be able to choose God, there had to be at least one *not*-God option. Hence that darned tree, the tree of the knowledge of good and evil.

God or *not*-God?

Eve? Adam?

We know what they chose. Thankfully, our God is a merciful God of many chances—One who forgives and makes a way for all sinners (even the very first ones) to find their way back to Him. Even though God knew His beloved creation wouldn't choose Him in that garden, He never stops choosing us. He is relentless in His great love for us, and He has a beautiful plan that was written before He created the universe.

Someday all the tears will dry up and all the pain will be eliminated. Someday our enemy, that serpent of old, will have his last hurrah, and those who have chosen God by choosing to believe in and accept the free gift of His Son, Jesus, will be in paradise, where we were meant to be all along.

IN THE MEANTIME

In the meantime, while we wait for that heavenly day, God is always loving us. He loved us before we ever gave Him a second thought. He loves us when we fail. He loves us warts and all. Even when we don't feel it or receive it. Beyond amazing! Oh, what a God!

I'm convinced that one of the hardest things to do is to receive. Isn't it so much easier to give someone else a gift than to accept one? Why are we like that? Why are we so goofy? I'm not totally sure. But I do know that the crazy, awkward feeling we get when someone tries to bring us a meal or do something special just for us is somehow working its way into our relationship with God.

We put up walls that keep God's love out. We list reasons why we don't deserve His love. We're eager to do things *for* God, but hesitant to accept His unconditional love. Why?

The reasons are many, but I'll bet it boils down to this: We're wounded people. And we've wounded each other. We've let each other down. We've been poor examples of love with skin on, which makes it harder for anyone to understand a love they can't see. And though humanity has dropped the love ball, we can't help but blame God, accusing Him of being responsible for it all.

I'll bet it grieves God to no end. Not only because we're misperceiving Him, but because when we get God all wrong, we miss out on the very thing our hearts are aching for. We put our hands up in refusal of the very remedy—the only remedy—that can heal our broken hearts.

Enter Jesus.

After years of watching humanity miss the mark, the Father sends His Son to earth to help us understand and set a few things straight.

- He came to show us true servanthood.
- He modeled what it looks like to really love people, including those who don't seem to deserve love.
- He demonstrated how to be a true child of God and enjoy a continual relationship with the Father.
- He showed us what is meant by true sacrifice, and
- In His death on the cross, He expressed how ridiculously loved we are.

But that's not all. He came to reveal who the Father truly is.

Jesus answered: "Don't you know me Philip, even after I have been among you such a long time? Anyone who has seen me has seen the Father. How can you say, 'Show us the Father'? Don't you believe that I am in the Father, and that the Father is in me? The words I say to you I do not speak on my own authority. Rather, it is the Father, living in me, who is doing his work." (John 14:9-10)

I'm going to take some liberty and paraphrase just a bit here. It's like Jesus is saying: "If you want to know what your heavenly Father is like, look at Me. When you look at My life—the things I do, the things I say, the way I treat people, the way I feel about you—you have seen the Father. When you see My heart, you're seeing His." God came to earth with flesh on so we could see Him more clearly. So we could see how much He loves us and get a preview of the good things to come if we say yes to Him.

When we doubt the goodness or the greatness of our God—when we wonder why in the world it's such a great thing to be a God-glorifier—all we need to do is read the New Testament Gospels and marvel at the kindness, gentleness, love, and power we see in the life of Jesus. In Him the fullness of the Godhead is on display, up close and personal (Colossians 2:9).

GOOD ENOUGH FOR JESUS

I want to close this chapter by mentioning one of the main reasons I think it's pretty amazing to be a God-glorifier: it's exactly what Jesus was. If glorifying the Father was good enough for Jesus, then it surely can be good enough for us.

Look at a few of the things Jesus said about Himself during His earthly ministry:

- *Very truly I tell you, the Son can do nothing by himself; he can do only what he sees his Father doing, because whatever the Father does the Son also does.* (John 5:19)
- *For the Father loves the Son and shows him all he does. Yes, and he will show him even greater works than these, so that you will be amazed.* (John 5:20)
- *By myself I can do nothing; I judge only as I hear, and my judgment is just, for I seek not to please myself but him who sent me.* (John 5:30)

- *For I did not speak on my own, but the Father who sent me commanded me to say all that I have spoken.* (John 12:49)
- *I no longer call you servants, because a servant does not know his master's business. Instead, I have called you friends, for everything that I learned from my Father I have made known to you.* (John 15:15)

Jesus was quite clear: He came to earth to make the Father known. He revealed what He knew of the Father (which was everything). He spoke the words the Father told Him to speak. He did only what the Father told Him to do. He mirrored the Father perfectly.

He knew who the Father was, and He made Him known to anyone who would listen. That's exactly what we're here to do too. To experience all we can of our heavenly Father and then reflect Him to the world.

When we follow our beautiful leader, Jesus, we will find ourselves living our beautiful purpose. And the lives of those we come in contact with will be touched in ways that will make them want to know the God we serve. When this happens, we'll be more than glad to tell them, because that's what we do. It's a glorious cycle of purpose.

If you have one of those old WWJD bracelets collecting dust in a junk drawer somewhere, you might think about putting it on again. Only this time, think of it with our new, purpose-driven perspective: What would Jesus do? He would glorify the Father.

So can we.

HOW ABOUT YOU?

1) How do you truly feel about being a God-glorifier? Be honest.

2) What do you think might cause you or someone else to feel disappointed or let down by the primary purpose for which we were created?

3) What things have happened in your life or in the world around you that demonstrate God's goodness?

4) What do you love most about Jesus? What does this reveal about your heavenly Father?

POINTS ON PURPOSE:

» The more we know about how amazing God is, the more amazing our primary purpose becomes. Nature itself gives us some pretty incredible evidence for the greatness of God.

Add to that His unconditional love for us when we deserve it the least, and glorifying God proves to be a tremendous reason for being alive.

» Jesus Himself had the purpose of glorifying the Father. He came to make the Father easier to see and to model how to make Him known. If glorifying the Father was good enough for Jesus, I'd say we're in incredible company.

CHAPTER EIGHT

PURPOSE
YOUR WAY

All vacuums aren't the same, and neither are all God-glorifiers.

Even though all vacuums are dirt-suckers, they specialize in many different tasks. Some vacuums are made for upholstery. Others are made for use on construction sites, where they suck up nails and other debris along with dirt. Some vacuums are even able to take in water with their dirt.

All vacuums have the manufacturer-given, primary purpose of sucking up dirt. But they've also been given an individualized purpose, so that they may do it in a particular way or setting. So it is with us (although in infinitely multiplied and far more complex variety). Even though all of humanity has been given the same primary purpose, we've also been given a *personal purpose:* a specialized way in which we will individually glorify God best. Once we know our primary purpose, we will want to put some thought into figuring out our personal purpose. Not so we can lay claim to our amazing skills and talents for an ego boost, but so we can glorify God better, with more precision.

Think of it this way: You can take a dust buster to a construction site and, yes, it will do a tiny little bit of good. But when you take that same dust buster to the laundry room to tackle the sand that fell out of your child's beach towel . . . watch out! That little instrument will shine. It doesn't matter to the dust buster that the laundry room is its playing field. It's just happy to be in the right place at the right time, perfectly made for the job!

That's a great way for us to view the importance of our personal purpose. Identifying it is only going to make us better able to glorify God—better able to introduce a hurting and dying world to its Savior and King.

HOW DO WE FIND IT?

Here's where all the books, blogs, and quizzes come in handy. There are resources galore out there, developed for the sole purpose of helping us figure out what we're good at. Most any book that has *purpose* or *calling* in the title is likely to include a method by which people can discern their special skillsets.

There's no problem whatsoever with using resources like these to figure a few things out. Just beware the temptation to blur the lines again, to mistake *calling* for *purpose* and, more specifically, *personal purpose* for *primary purpose*. Hopefully by now, you're beginning to see the important distinctions.

In general, I think most of the quizzes and books give us similar instructions. They suggest good things like this:

- Identify what you enjoy spending your time doing (writing, exercise, helping the elderly, teaching, building, cooking, nature, etc.).

- Look back on your life to see what situations you've found yourself in repeatedly (counseling friends through crisis, solving problems others can't seem to solve, researching the latest books on certain subjects and applying their conclusions in real-world ways, cheering others on, leading groups or teams, making others feel welcome, etc.).

- Determine what you most definitely aren't good at and would never want to do.

- Pinpoint skills and talents—things you have a propensity for (music, writing, teaching, math, sales, farming, homemaking, etc.).

- Identify what you seem to get the opportunity to do most often.

- Assess the feedback you receive when you do the things you do: in what areas do you receive the best feedback? (For me, it's definitely not my cooking!)

All of these things point to your personal purpose.

Looking at our lives with such openness and honesty will be a great help in figuring out the unique ways God has equipped us to glorify Him. But while we're trying to discern this, let's not quit moving. The most important thing we will ever do is to continue to receive God's love and then pay it forward. And what's sweet is, while we focus on the loving, God continues to light the way.

Author John Burke says it this way: "How do we know our unique [personal] purpose? It always starts with loving and seeking God, then following his lead to love the people closest to us, and then using the gifts and passions He's put in us to serve humanity. You don't need to worry about not fulfilling your purpose; if you seek God and His will, you will live it. But we can't forget, it's all about love."[1]

IN REAL LIFE

Let's get a glimpse of what all this looks like in real lives.

First, there's my literary agent, Wayne. Early in his Christian life, he attended a seminar that focused on finding a mission. That conference got him thinking about his talents and skills, and also praying about what he should do with them. After much prayer and contemplation, God dropped a mission in his heart—one that was perfectly suited to his skillset. God urged Wayne to "put life-changing materials into the hands of people who need them." Wayne knew that one of the main ways he would glorify God from that point on was by using his unique know-how and interests to resource people. He would help them get the books and teachings they'd need in order to better understand and follow God.

This is quite different than a pinpoint, specific calling. *Where?* *When?* and *How?* weren't included in the directive. But that's okay. We don't have to have those answers to discern our personal purpose; God will direct the details in His timing.

Once Wayne knew his *personal purpose,* he set about resourcing people as opportunities opened up for him, and this is what he told me about it: "Whether I'm writing or selling or publishing books, I think of those people who need them. It's not about my *doing;* it's about being open to God's leading and letting Him bring the harvest."

Wayne knows his purpose: first, to glorify God with His life; and second, to glorify God by identifying and putting quality resources in people's hands. Living these two things one day at a time has led to many exciting opportunities for him. And the wonderful thing is, he never had to stress or worry about it. When God wanted to use him in a certain place, He called.

Another beautiful example is my friend and editor, Kris. She is one of those rare people whose passion is to help others fulfill their passions. She has known since her twenties that her personal purpose is to use her unique skills "to set up people to succeed." She is a lifter, lifting others so they can keep reaching higher.

Kris recognizes that her primary purpose is to glorify God, but she is extremely gifted with words and communication. And she loves others—their hearts and their words—as the devoted mentor she is. God has allowed her to combine these callings—mentoring and crafting words—to, among other things, help more people than I can say write and publish books and Bibles that enable readers to live more effectively, more intentionally, for the Lord. She does it one purpose-full day at a time.

In my own life, I figured out that my personal purpose centers around honest communication and connecting others to the heart of God. As I look back over my entire life, I can recall many situations in which I had a desire to just cut through the superficial and talk about the real. Even in high school, I was often deemed the Debbie Downer of parties because I was "too serious." When other friends wanted to talk about fashion or which couples looked cute together, I wanted to talk about feelings and the meaning of life.

I've always been a talker, and I've always loved writing. After becoming a Christian, I still loved to talk—only I started talking a lot about Jesus. And I couldn't learn enough about Him either, which leads to another thing I've always had a passion for: academics (yes, I'm a book nerd). Because of my love of honest communication and learning, I ended up getting a teaching degree and then teaching language arts (writing and grammar) in the public schools for several years.

At church, I often ended up teaching in the children's ministry, and over the years I was asked to share at women's Bible studies. Can you begin to see an overarching theme? God has given me a love of reading, learning, writing, and communicating. I've had repeated opportunities to do all of those things in varying degrees over the years, and have received positive feedback along the way (with constructive feedback too, of course).

God has never put me in a marching band or an a capella group or anything related to singing or playing a musical instrument. Hence, I will not be glorifying God on tour with Jeremy

Camp, no matter what my inner worship gal thinks. And that's just fine. I'm perfectly content to leave the harmonizing to my friends who can "sang" (this is how we say it in the South), and be about glorifying God in the custom ways He's purposed me for.

WE ALL HAVE A MINISTRY

Most often when we hear the word *ministry,* we picture efforts like youth ministry, or homeless ministry, or worship ministry. We're thinking of vocations that originate within—or are associated with—a particular church. And we admire those people who work *in the ministry.* Which is a good thing. People who work in churches need our love and support. They often put in far more hours than anyone truly knows, and they carry a lot of silent burdens. Please always pray for those who formally serve your church.

But, don't be tricked into thinking they are the only ones who work *in the ministry.*

We all do. We are all ministers. Any Christian who is following Christ is a minister, an ambassador, a witness for Jesus. The Bible tells us this. Take a look:

- *All this is from God, who reconciled us to himself through Christ and gave us the ministry of reconciliation.* (2 Corinthians 5:18)

- *We are therefore Christ's ambassadors, as though God were making his appeal through us.* (2 Corinthians 5:20a)

- *You will receive power when the Holy Spirit comes on you; and you will be my witnesses in Jerusalem, and in all Judea and Samaria, and to the ends of the earth.* (Acts 1:8)

It's pretty clear that we are all needed out there in the world to help hurting and lost people find their way back home. And even though some hurting people do end up finding their way to an actual church, many of them don't. However, they might find their way to your workplace or neighborhood. Which is why ministry can't happen only in churches.

There are hurting people at the grocery store, at the bank, working in the computer industry, making tires, baking bread, homeschooling, cleaning homes—you name it—who need the love and truth of Jesus. And we can deliver it. When we do, we must remember: It's not the delivery address that matters most; it's what we're delivering. It's what's inside us that has the value, not *where* we are.

To illustrate: What's so valuable about a box of diamonds? Is it where the box is, or what's inside the box? What's inside, right? That box of diamonds is extremely valuable no matter where it goes. Likewise, what's most important is what we carry with us everywhere we go. Our God is most important, and where we go, He goes.

Christian philosopher J. P. Moreland says:

A vocation includes a job, but it is much, much more. It is the specific role I am to play in life, and it includes the sum total of the natural talents, spiritual gifts, and historical circumstances providentially bestowed on me by God. An important part of a believer's vocation is his or her major in college or main form of work as a career. If we are to be integrated, holistic Christians who make an impact on the world, we need to learn how to be Christian doctors, schoolteachers, businesspersons, and so forth.[2]

If you're a stay-at-home mom, or the owner of a small business, or a schoolteacher, or a police officer, or whatever it is you do . . . the body of Christ needs you. Yes, you. It takes each and every one of us to bring God's glory to the earth, because God has ordained things to work that way.

First Corinthians 10:31 says, "So whether you eat or drink or whatever you do, do it all for the glory of God." Whatever we're doing can be done to the glory of God. Even our eating and drinking, which is great news for foodies.

THE WORD OF YOUR TESTIMONY

In addition to using our various ministries, God will use us uniquely through our testimony. Your testimony is your story—a combination of things that have happened in your life and how you've related to God along the way. People love stories.

Over the years I've heard many testimonies, and some of them I'll never forget. Just think about the ones that stood out most to you. What was so special about them? What made them memorable?

When I ask my middle and high school Bible students what they think makes a testimony powerful, they typically mention the ones that include the most depraved beginnings: stories of people who used to be drug addicts or criminals but who eventually came to Christ. Even among their peers, they believe the students with the best testimonies are those who've done the worst things and then accepted God's forgiveness. In my students' minds, the bad stuff is what makes the testimony good.

We adults fall into that trap too. And the enemy loves it because it keeps many of us silent. We think our testimony is boring if we've pretty much walked the straight and narrow. I mean, who wants to hear a story about a good Christian boy who grew up without using cuss words, went to college without attending one frat party, and eventually became a Christian banker? Vanilla with a capital *V*, right?

Wrong. All wrong.

You see, the power in your testimony is not the depths of your former depravity. The power is the authenticity of your relationship with God today.

I'll admit, hearing about all the hell someone has been through in his or her life is riveting at times, but it has no more power than some daytime talk show if it's not backed by a life that is truly bearing the fruit of heaven in the day to day. The real fireworks come from evidence of God's love and healing touch bursting through our humanness.

It's not our past that people need; it's our present. What we know and live by today because we've tasted and seen God's truth, faithfulness, and hope.

Revelation 12:11 tells us: "They triumphed over him by the blood of the Lamb and by the word of their testimony; they did not love their lives so much as to shrink from death." God's Word says we overcome the enemy by the blood of Christ and our story, not by reliving our sinful past.

It's not the evil stuff that defeats the evil one. What overcomes Satan is the victory we're walking in. Sure, we might mention a bit of our past in order to show we're relatable—that we understand certain people groups or situations. But the good stuff in our stories is the God stuff. The love, joy, peace, and hope that we've accessed and are experiencing in our lives. The pay dirt is what's all about *Him*.

That's what the world wants most. It's what people need. They need hope. They need love. They need God.

And we have Him.

Whatever measure of victory you're walking in today, *there* is the power of your testimony. Even if you never smoked one cigarette or broke any rules, your testimony kicks the devil's rear if you have a genuine, life-giving relationship with the Lord today. If you *really* have joy no matter what's going on in your world. If you *really* have hope despite the negativity that surrounds you. If you *really* see your beauty no matter what the scale says. If you *really* feel secure regardless of how many Facebook followers you can claim or how much money's in the bank.

It's our *really* that matters, because it's only what we really have that we can offer to others.

To have a powerful testimony, we must put our all into our today and get more of God. We must never stop pursuing the freedom, healing, and love Jesus died to bring us. Each day we must be open like David was when he prayed: "Search me, God, and know my heart; test me and know my anxious thoughts. See if there is any offensive way in me, and lead me in the way everlasting" (Psalm 139:23–24).

We want God's light to shine in every dark place, including our own hearts, so we can eyeball the obstacles we've been tripping over—what self-defeating cycles we may have been caught in—and get free. As all the clutter is removed, we might just be able to see more clearly the talents and gifts He's given us as one-of-a-kind glorifiers of Him.

HOW ABOUT YOU?

1) Skye Jethani has written: "The call to live in continual communion with God means that every person's life, no matter how mundane, is elevated to sacred heights."[3]

   a) Are there times when you feel that your life is mundane?

   b) What does this quote suggest can turn the mundane into the sacred?

2) What clues can you see as to what your personal purpose might be?

3) If you aren't sure about your personal purpose yet, what information do you feel you still need? What's your plan to secure that information?

4) In your own words, explain why we don't need a "special" calling in order to live a life of purpose.

POINTS ON PURPOSE:

» Even though we all have the same primary purpose to glorify God, we will each do that in unique ways. Just as there are many different types of vacuums, there are many different types of God-glorifiers. He's given each of us varying skills and gifts to be used exactly where He wants us.

» Every one of us is needed to spread God's glory throughout the earth, which means we all have a ministry. Ministry isn't just for people who work at a church or a parachurch organization. God will use the testimony of our daily life— His victories and *real* presence in our now—to draw those around us to Himself.

CHAPTER NINE

LIKE AN
AREA RUG

The red carpet. Three little words that, without any further description whatsoever, make something inside of us stand at attention and use proper grammar.

We all know what it is, that ruby runway. I'll bet if you close your eyes right now, you can see it with crystal clarity. And on it you can see all the beautiful people dressed in designer clothing being ushered into exclusive and ritzy places.

No other carpet demands such respect. And yet no other is quite so deceptive. Perhaps its dark side has to do with its origins.

The crimson carpet is thought to have made its debut around 458 BC in the Greek tragedy *Agamemnon* by Aeschylus. In this mesmerizing tale of love and war, a beautiful queen gets word that her husband, the king, is returning safely home from battle. To honor him, she spreads a crimson carpet for him alone to walk on, leading from his chariot to the palace door. Once she sees the king, she waves and bids him a warm *Welcome home.* He proudly takes the specially appointed path, enjoying the effort his bride has put into celebrating his return. He walks through the grand entrance, gets settled in . . . and then she kills him.

Yes, folks. That much-lauded red carpet had its start as a pathway to death. And though it's a logical fallacy to say that "because the origin of something is evil, every permutation of the thing is also evil," I do think a remnant of the original deception is found in our modern rendition.

I just can't help seeing the trap in it. Our deep-seated desire for that red roll of polyester fibers has all the lure of a gleaming yellow brick road laid out in front of us, wooing us to keep dreaming, keep hoping, keep striving. And for what? For the day when the magical carpet of wonders will finally be rolled out just for us?

ONE LONG LINE OF RED

I don't know if it's because we live in the age of participation awards, when every kid on the team gets a trophy just for having a pulse and bringing snacks when their turn arrives, but somehow we've come to believe we all have a red-carpet calling coming. And when it comes, it will be spectacular. *Dooo ta doooo!* A trumpet will sound first, then an angel with a voice like Bob Barker will declare: "Beloved Teasi, come on down! You're the next recipient of a special calling! Your day has finally come—the moment everything's been all about! Here it is. Walk ye in it!"

But is that how it's really going to happen for most of us? Does it happen this way for *anyone*?

If so, I've never seen it. Yes, I've seen people get more breaks than others, and I've seen people who seem to have had a pretty easy time making their way into a ministry role or career path. But I think if we could glance behind the curtain into their real lives, we'd witness plenty of desperate prayers, days of struggle, and lots of tears. I don't believe there's anyone who lives full-time on Easy Street.

Even if it could happen this way, what would the rest of our days be like? Would everything from that point on seem anticlimactic, or would we expect each day to surpass the exhilaration of the red-carpet moment? Could anything compare? Would we need the trumpets to continually sound in order to feel alive? Would the carpet have to be rolled out again and again in order for us to feel satisfied?

And if we could get a red-carpet moment every day of our lives—if from that moment on, our daily walk was one of miles and miles of narrow, red, and nothing-but-red carpet—would we really like it?

I don't know about you, but I know myself well enough to safely say I'd be sick of it soon enough. Even the epic would become mundane. I think this is why we see so much pain and suffering in the lives of the rich and famous, don't you? That crimson carpet can become a pathway to death no matter who walks it.

A BEAUTIFUL AREA RUG

I think God has something much more glorious in mind for us. Instead of rolling out endless miles of red carpet that looks exactly the same for everyone, I truly believe God has rolled out a wonderfully unique, handcrafted area rug for each and every one of us. We all get our own, and not one looks like any other.

Let's think about area rugs for a minute. They've been around for thousands of years, and many of them are full of history and beauty. Some are quite ornate and valuable. One seventeenth-century Persian rug actually sold for $9.5 million! Can you imagine? And did you know that during the Middle Ages, when knights were knighted, they knelt on a special hand-crafted rug made just for the occasion? It became one of their most prized possessions, serving for the rest of their lives as a reminder of a deeply meaningful part of their very identity.

What if that's what God does for us? What if He has handcrafted a very special area rug for each of us? What if the beauty and power and even the identity of our lives is woven into its fibers? And what if we've been missing all that beauty because we've been too busy watching the horizon for the arrival of that ridiculous red carpet?

If so, what do you think would happen if we stopped horizon gazing? What if we switched everything up and started taking a good, long look at the area rug we've been on all along? I wonder how things might change?

THE BOUNDARY LINES

I started thinking about this area-rug concept shortly after a trip my family took to Oregon a few years ago. My husband grew up in Oregon, where my precious in-loves (no in-laws in our family) still live, and we try to visit as often as we can.

On that particular trip, we spent a full day with a farming family that my husband had worked for through his teen years. The day included my very first ride on a bean-picker. That experience was followed by a trip to a cannery in a truck loaded to the brim with beans. At one point we had to ride on a small river ferry in that heavy rig. I remember thinking, *What a ridiculous end this would be—death by drowning, with a million green beans!* Thankfully we all survived, and we spent the rest of the day hanging out, reminiscing about my husband's early days, sharing meals, and enjoying the simple things.

These folks are salt of the earth. Their every morning starts well before the sun comes up and ends in exhaustion after the sun has gone down. They work hard, pray at mealtimes, love their neighbors, laugh at ridiculous jokes, and smell like tractor grease. And I couldn't help but hunger to have what they have. Or, better yet . . . to *not* have what they didn't have: a life-sucking desire to figure out their special calling.

It was painfully obvious to me that these precious people were so busy working their land each day, and taking care of family and friends, that they didn't have time to seek prophetic words, make networking connections, build a platform, or increase their number of Facebook followers. I could see that even though they were exhausted from physical labor, they weren't exhausted like I was—they weren't tired from years of waiting for life to finally begin. No. Any fatigue they were feeling was due to actually *living*. They put their hands to the plow each and every day, working their land. And the simple beauty of it all made my heart ache.

I wanted land of my own to work. I wanted the simplicity of putting my hands to the plow right outside my back door and putting my head on the pillow each night, feeling the satisfaction of a good day's labor.

Shortly after that trip, I discovered this is exactly what God has in mind for all of us. We all have land—clearly defined land—to work.

PSALM 16

To see what I mean, let's look at Psalm 16 together.

> *A Miktam of David. Keep me safe, my God, for in you I take refuge. I say to the LORD, "You are my Lord; apart from you I have no good thing." I say of the holy people who are in the land, "They are the noble ones in whom is all my delight." Those who run after other gods will suffer more and more. I will not pour out libations of blood to such gods or take up their names on my lips. LORD, you alone are my portion and my cup; you make my lot secure. The boundary lines have fallen for me in pleasant places; surely I have a delightful inheritance. I will praise the LORD, who counsels me; even at night my heart instructs me. I keep my eyes always on the LORD. With him at my right hand, I will not be shaken. Therefore my heart is glad and my tongue rejoices; my body also will rest secure, because*

you will not abandon me to the realm of the dead, nor will you let your faithful one see decay. You make known to me the path of life; you will fill me with joy in your presence, with eternal pleasures at your right hand.

I discovered some amazing treasure within the words of this psalm when I really started looking. One interesting detail is that odd word at the very beginning: *miktam.* There aren't many psalms that start this way—maybe only a handful. And I read in a couple of places that, although the exact meaning is debated, it was a word sometimes used in ancient days to denote something of distinct importance, something worth more than gold and worth engraving upon a lasting stone. Consequently, some call this a *Golden Psalm.*

Whether or not *miktam* denotes anything special, this psalm is special enough to be referred to by both Peter (Acts 2:22–32) and Paul (Acts 13:32–38) in the New Testament. Both writers make the point that parts of the message are actually more about Jesus than about David. After all, they say, David actually did die and "see decay." The one to whom these verses more accurately refer is none other than Jesus, who bodily came out of the grave and who now sits at the right hand of God the Father.

Parts of this psalm are, in fact, prophetic—perhaps even describing the very prayers of Christ before He was to be crucified. Remember His words regarding a *cup* in the garden? "Father, if you are willing, remove this cup from me. Nevertheless, not my will, but yours, be done" (Luke 22:42). Reminds me of what David wrote in verse 5: "LORD, you alone are my portion and my cup; you make my lot secure."

The point I'm getting at, though I'll admit theologians disagree on the strength of the connection here, is that Christ Himself knew this psalm and knew that He was the fulfillment of it. He also understood that His heavenly Father had drawn pleasant lines for Him that entailed every aspect of His earthly life, including the suffering. *The boundary lines laid for His life* were in pleasant places because they were drawn by His Father, and He knew the Father's heart perfectly.

So what does this have to do with us? I'm glad you asked.

Before I get back to our area-rug discussion, I want to share one more treasure I discovered in my study of Psalm 16. One that I hope you'll recognize as a treasure for you too.

The scholars who study the literary forms found in the Bible have identified patterns and techniques ancient writers used in order to emphasize certain things *and* make them easier to memorize. Because people in ancient times lived in a pre-literate, predominantly oral culture, it was necessary to keep the main thing the main thing and highlight what was important.

One of the techniques used was a *chiastic pattern*. A chiastic pattern might have looked something like this: *A-B-C-C-B-A*. It's like a mirrored set, where the first and last elements reflect one another, reiterating and potentially strengthening each other's meaning, and the middle elements reflect, and so on. The center point might have significance as well.

You can sometimes find this pattern in segments of Scripture, and some experts say you can find this pattern in Psalms 15—24. I can definitely see it. If you take the time to read these psalms, I think you will notice that Psalm 15 and 24 have a common theme and add something to each other. The same is true of the other pairs: 16 and 23; 17 and 22; 18 and 21; 19 and 20.

I'm not sure if you've tuned in to it already, but Psalm 16 would be paired with Psalm 23. Just in case you don't remember that one, let's look at it again, in the ESV translation:

> *A Psalm of David. The LORD is my shepherd; I shall not want. He makes me lie down in green pastures. He leads me beside still waters. He restores my soul. He leads me in paths of righteousness for his name's sake. Even though I walk through the valley of the shadow of death, I will fear no evil, for you are with me; your rod and your staff, they comfort me. You prepare a table before me in the presence of my enemies; you anoint my head with oil; my cup overflows. Surely goodness and mercy shall follow me all the days of my life, and I shall dwell in the house of the LORD forever.*

This is certainly among the best-known psalms, and we cling to it when life is at its toughest—when days are darkest, and we need a reminder that God's got us . . . that He has a plan for us, even in the chaos and pain. It reminds us that the Lord is our provider and our all. That He has green pastures and still waters and paths of righteousness prepared for us. It kind of sounds a little like "The lines have fallen for me in pleasant places; indeed, I have a beautiful inheritance." That's the key verse in Psalm 16. It's verse 6, which just happens to be right in the middle of it all.

I'm not sure how we can read these two psalms and not get this message: God has drawn the boundary lines of our lives, and He intends to fill them with good and pleasant things. Within those boundary lines, we will find all we need because there we are in His will. There we shall discover what we were meant to discover all along: That He alone is our portion and our cup. Our *everything*. He is our Shepherd, and when we rest in this, we shall not want.

OUR AREA RUGS

So, what are the boundary lines in our lives today? How can you figure out what your area rug looks like?

First, I'd recommend praying about it, asking God. After all, He's the One who sets the edges of your "territory": "And he made from one man every nation of mankind to live on all the face of the earth, having determined allotted periods and the boundaries of their dwelling place" (Acts 17:26). Pray that God will begin to show you anything you've been missing—the things that have been within your clearly defined territory all along. And start with the easy stuff that you can quickly identify, like:

- The four walls you live within
- The parents and siblings that are yours
- The spouse that is yours (if you have one)
- The children that belong to you (if any)
- The neighborhood you live in
- The job you have now
- The talents and skillsets you have
- The people you call "friend"
- The church you attend
- The hobbies you enjoy

- The opportunities right in front of you
- The twenty-four hours in which you are living and breathing

As you survey these obvious lines, others might come into focus. You begin to see things you've never seen before, and value things you've never valued. I'll give you an example from my life.

I taught middle-school English for several years. I loved my students, but I'll admit, there were many days I left in tears because of the classroom management issues I dealt with. I poured my heart and soul into loving those kids and teaching them some grammar skills, but I'd arrive home empty. Very empty.

When the time came that I felt God calling me to write my first book, I quit my teaching job and wrote. Then I was given some opportunities to speak at a few women's retreats. I thought *for sure* my classroom teaching days were over. In fact, I'm a little ashamed to say, I would have considered going back into the classroom a major concession—three giant steps back and miles away from the budding speaking and writing career I *just knew* would be my red carpet.

But . . . when God started teaching me about my area rug and showing me all the beautiful, life-giving benefits to living with purpose in view instead of calling, I took a closer look around me. Rather than squinting at the horizon for opportunities I was *hoping* might come someday, I decided to take note of what was on my area rug *today*. What were the things within my realm of possibility? Where could I serve NOW? And teaching at my sons' Christian school was within the borders of my area rug. Teaching middle-school Bible and language arts . . . in a classroom *(gasp)*.

What's amazing about it is this: by that time, it no longer felt like a concession whatsoever, thanks to my new understanding and perspective. In fact, it was glorious. And to this day, as I sit writing this book, I'm teaching there. I started my day by teaching Bible to two classes of tenth graders. Glorious. I mean, fulfilling to the max.

As a God-magnifier whose personal purpose is to glorify Him by connecting others' hearts to His, and who has been called to doing that through teaching during this season in my life, it doesn't matter to me whether I'm instructing a small group of precious sixth-grade girls, or a room full of goofy high schoolers, or a stadium full of women. The fulfillment comes in simply being on my area rug, living as the woman God made me to be, loving the people who are right in front of me to love.

SOME THINGS WE MIGHT HAVE MISSED

When we disregard or diminish the importance of the things God has placed within the boundary lines of our own lives—those things that can be found on our area rug—other people pay the price. This is just another reason God wants us to quit looking to the horizon, or even at other people's area rugs. He needs us all right where we are.

I know not all of us are parents, or even want to be, but I'd like to take a moment to stress how significant this thread of the area rug is for those of us who are. The impact of kids being raised without a father or mother is heart-wrenching. Please, please don't ever devalue that one priceless role you play.

Look at some of the statistics regarding children raised without a father:

- Nearly 65 percent of youth suicides are from fatherless homes—five times the average.
- 90 percent of all homeless and runaway children are from fatherless homes—thirty-two times the average.
- 85 percent of all children who exhibit behavioral disorders come from fatherless homes—twenty times the average.
- 80 percent of rapists come from fatherless homes—fourteen times the average.
- 71 percent of all high school dropouts come from fatherless homes—nine times the average.[1]

This is only a tiny sample of the accumulating evidence reflecting the negative impact of a fatherless home.

And moms, your role is huge too. Several studies have shown how essential a mother's love and nurturing are in a child's development. The kids who grow up without a mom (whether she is physically or emotionally absent) have a much harder time learning to trust, building healthy relationships, and feeling secure in general. They often battle depression at greater rates than children raised with a mother, and it's not uncommon for them to deal with a myriad of mental health issues throughout life.[2]

Mom, when you are up all night rocking that baby while every other person in the neighborhood is sound asleep, when you are kissing boo boos and wiping away tears, you are doing far more than just that. You are building a person; you are watering a soul. Even more, you are being "God's love with skin on" for the next generation of kingdom warriors. That thread woven into your area rug is critical. Please don't ever feel *less than* when you're mothering.

And for all of us, whether we're parents or not, here's a statistic we can do something about. In most churches you will find an unfortunate principle at play, the Pareto Principle, which generally states that 20 percent of what gets invested produces 80 percent of the results.[3] Applied in a church setting, it means that 20 percent of the people do 80 percent of the work. Your congregation may have better numbers, but if you've ever worked at a church or known someone who does, you're aware that the stats are pretty accurate. Churches are usually in desperate need of more volunteers.

Why is this? There are several factors, but I have a theory. I wonder if the scarcity of active volunteers is because many of us are still waiting for our magnificent calling, and we can't be bothered with the "little" things? Perhaps when the pastor gets up and pleads for help with the children, or urges people to get involved in the church's hospitality ministries, maybe these aren't big enough. And maybe we're afraid to get involved in these "lesser" service opportunities for fear that we'll be so busy doing those, we'll miss our real calling when it finally comes around.

Again, it's just my theory, but sadly it's been true of me at different times in the past. Hearing that desperate plea for a few more hands in the kitchen, or some loving folks to play with toddlers,

I've suddenly become far too busy (or needy or tired or depressed or . . . you name it) for things like that.

Think what might happen in our churches if everyone would decide to put their hands to the plow with what's right there on their own area rug! Rather than waiting to be asked to speak from the pulpit, why don't you go speak to the five-year-olds that are in class with *your* five-year-old? Rather than waiting for an invitation to head up the benevolence ministry, why not rustle up a team of friends—or maybe even your small group—to help organize the food pantry and deliver food to those in need? I think you'll be surprised how fulfilled you'll start to feel. And I'll just warn you now: it can be addictive.

I love this reminder from Ravi Zacharias: "The Bible is full of stories about incredible leaders rescued in very dramatic settings—Moses, Paul, Daniel, and others. The same is true in church history: think of John Wesley, Blaise Pascal, and countless others. But we must recognize that it does not always happen that way, and God can call us by slow, encouraging methods as well as by dramatic ones."[4]

A FLYING CARPET

One of the fun parts of living on your area rug—being content to enjoy what God has hand-sewn into all the different aspects of your life—is that He can turn that area rug into a flying carpet anytime He wants to. And that, my friends, is a calling.

All the different places and exact scenarios God takes us in order for us to do the kind of glorifying we're made to do? Those are our callings. Sometimes we will find ourselves called to a completely different set of circumstances than we've known before, yet find ourselves using the same unique skill-set God has gifted us with. My husband, whose passion is infrastructure and empowering others to shine, is a great example. For years he worked diligently on his area rug as a farm manager for a country music icon. His job required him to manage a variety of things, including people, equipment, land, and livestock. He did everything from animal care to architectural design, but his main joy was knowing that what he did allowed his boss to do what she did without the stress of worrying about her estate.

After fifteen years of working there, God turned his area rug into a flying carpet, placing Bill in our home church as the children's pastor. He is using many of the exact same skills there. He manages people by leading and serving several full- and part-time staff along with hundreds of children's ministry volunteers. He manages the purchase and care of all the equipment they use, and he oversees the spiritual "feeding" of the "animals"—I mean, children. I'm just kidding. I adore children.

One thing that hasn't changed a bit between the two settings is Bill's desire to help others shine. He loves paving the way for his department heads to excel at what they do. And he loves supporting the ministry of the pastoral leadership in our church. Most importantly, he loves making God shine. My husband's true boss is his heavenly Father, and it's obvious in everything Bill does. He is fulfilling his primary and personal purpose through this specific calling, just as he was in the previous season as a farm manager.

Let's look again at how it all fits together:

1) We live aware that we are God-glorifiers who are getting to know Him more and more each day, which makes us even further excited about our primary purpose.

2) We learn to enjoy the personal purpose God has given us by using our God-given talents and skills where we can on our area rug each day—nothing is too small, no place too ordinary.

3) God calls us to different places and situations whenever He wants to, turning that area rug into a flying carpet.

4) We go along for the ride.

Let's get busy enjoying what's in front of us today, loving people right here and right now. Then, no matter if God keeps us where we are or sends us someplace new, it won't matter. We'll be completely fulfilled either way.

GOD'S BEAUTIFUL PAINTING

Imagine one last thing with me before we leave this chapter. Think of God's kingdom as a big, beautiful painting in process. Think of each of us as paintbrushes of different sizes and types, to be used for specific purposes until the moment the final stroke of paint is applied, when Jesus returns for us.

When we look at our lives this way, the most important thing is that the painting gets completed. We don't care what brush is used to create any particular part of this masterpiece; we just want to see God's masterpiece in its final form. We want the painting done! The sooner we can see Jesus face to face, the better.

If I've given you more analogies than you can manage, please forgive me. I'm sure not everyone is as inspired by word pictures as I am. But, I hope you feel encouraged by the main point, and that is: Be free, friend. Be free to live today; to live *your* day, in your place, with your skillset, with your amazing God. When you do, you can join our brother Paul in declaring, "I am not saying this because I am in need, for I have learned to be content whatever the circumstances. I know what it is to be in need, and I know what it is to have plenty. I have learned the secret of being content in any and every situation, whether well fed or hungry, whether living in plenty or in want. I can do all this through him who gives me strength" (Philippians 4:11–13).

HOW ABOUT YOU?

1) What are some of the clear boundary lines you can pinpoint in your life today?

2) Name at least one thing you see on your area rug that you may have been overlooking or devaluing.

3) How does the thought of enjoying your area rug make you feel?

4) Record your takeaways from these words by Ravi Zacharias:

A calling is simply God's shaping of your burden and beckoning you to your service to Him in the place and pursuit of His choosing. Finding your home in your service to Christ is key to noticing the threads designed just for you. It gives you that hand-in-glove sensation and provides the security of knowing that you are utilizing your gifts and your will to God's ends first, not for you. When your will becomes aligned with God's will, His calling upon you has found its home.[5]

POINTS ON PURPOSE:

» Although the thought of a red-carpet calling seems grand, God's desire is for us to enjoy the ornate area rug He has handcrafted for each of us. Our area rug is defined by the pleasant boundary lines He has set in place for us—boundary lines that are easy to see if we prayerfully look at our lives.

» As we take full advantage of the beautiful opportunities that are on our area rugs, with an eye toward loving God and people right where we are today, God can turn our area rug into a flying carpet anytime He wants and move us to a different place—a different calling—whenever He chooses.

But it's all up to Him. We will be just as content here or there because our fulfillment comes from glorifying Him no matter where we are.

CHAPTER TEN

PURPOSEFULLY EVER AFTER

Have you ever lost your keys and then lost precious time looking for them? It's so frustrating, isn't it? When it happens to me, one of the first things I do is retrace my steps. I try to remember the last time I had the keys in my hand. It works almost every time.

Nowadays, technology offers us even more assistance with finding things that we lose, especially our phones. The older I get, the more thankful I am for *anything* that can help me find missing things. Especially when what I've suddenly lost hold of is God's truth.

It's happened more often than I can count. I've had an incredible time with the Lord, read something that hit me right where I am, experienced God's love and power, journaled my takeaways, set my mind toward freedom and new mercies, and then . . . I walk into my day and somehow forget.

What I've learned from times like these is that I have to be even more intentional about holding tightly to my "valuables," and I have to do everything I can to prevent losing things. It's the same for us when it comes to remembering all we've learned about our life-changing primary purpose. We must hold tight to the truth, and we must take preventative steps to ensure that as we walk into each new day.

PREVENTATIVE MEASURE #1: HUMILITY

If you had to pick one animal that would most accurately represent *humility*, which one would you choose? A sweet, gentle Golden Retriever who's always ready to serve? A furry little rabbit just minding its own business while eating a tasty clover in your backyard? I would think of a strong and mighty stallion, rearing up on its hind legs with a majestic wave of its long and wild mane.

You might be wondering why. Why would I ask you to make this seemingly ridiculous decision in the first place, and then why, of all the animals in the world, would I pick a horse to represent humility?

The answer to the first question is: I'm just a little weird, and my mind sometimes makes goofy connections that occasionally make a good point. Answer number two is: I choose a strong and mighty stallion because of its power. Because humility is one of the single most powerful tools we have in our Christian walk, and . . . it's one of our most forceful and focused weapons against the schemes of our enemy.

We see humility in God's nature from the very start. Remember, we already saw that He actually humbled Himself enough to present Himself as an *option* in Eden. He allowed Adam and Eve to choose Him rather than simply making them do exactly what He wanted (which He most certainly could have done as a sovereign God). He chose to let us choose, and that is so important to remember.

We see God's humility even more distinctly in Christ's earthly life. The very fact that an infinite God with no limitations came to earth and lived with human limitations in order to help us see reality is incredible. Christ brought into view the reality of who we are and the reality of who God is. God the Father could have kept His Son in heaven and demanded that we figure it all out on our own, but that's just not who He is. He humbled Himself, forfeiting His own Son, so that we could have a living, breathing Person to show us how to live and be fulfilled in our God-glorifying purpose with the power that God supplies.

When we walk in humility, we tap into all of that and then some. We not only reflect God, but we attract His power. Look at this: "God opposes the proud, but gives grace to the humble" (James 4:6b ESV).

There are a couple of things I want to point out in this verse. First, we see that God is totally turned away by our pride. I'm not talking about the type of pride we feel when we're overwhelmed with affirmation toward our kid's accomplishments, or even the great things our country stands for. I'm talking about the pride that originates with the prideful one, Satan—the father of pride, of lies, and of all things *not*-God. This is the kind of pride that leads to an inflated view of self and self-rule. It says, *God? What God? I'm the boss of me!* And it can manifest in tricky ways: in all different forms of self-focus such as self-absorption, self-adulation, and even self-pity. (Yes, when we think of ourselves as worthless or rejected or insignificant, it's pride. Because it's all about me. The focus and the answer originate in self, not in God.)

Humility is the opposite. When we live as exactly who we are, nothing more and nothing less, we are walking in humility. When we get up each morning and plant our feet on the floor knowing we are God's—we belong to Him, we are made by Him, and we are loved by Him—we are putting on humility. When we walk in the confidence that is ours in Christ, that's humility. So is claiming the full inheritance we've been given as co-heirs with Christ.

We are not doormats, and we are not gods. We are intricately created masterpieces in the hands of a Master Artist, living through Him, by Him, and for Him. When we live mindful of this, we attract God's grace because He loves humility.

James 4:6 tells us that God gives grace to the humble. That's a big, big deal. God's grace isn't simply His unmerited favor, as some may think. It's also His divine presence. And God tells us that our humility is what draws His divine presence into our situations.

Think of all the times in a day when you need God's presence. If you don't need it before you leave the house, you'll definitely need it the moment you come into contact with another human being. I often think it would be so much easier to stay righteous if there weren't any other people around! Yet there are, and we need each other, which is why we must have humility. It's neces-sary in order to maintain godly, peaceful, healthy relationships.

Walking in humility will help us stay focused on our primary purpose rather than our calling, because a big part of being hum-ble is being okay with staying low. I don't mean low like a door-mat. I mean low like *not on a high horse.* Low like *meek*—the oppo-site of haughty and lifted up. Low like *in a position of receiving and submitting* rather than calling all the shots.

In his powerful book *Humility* (which I highly recommend to everyone), Andrew Murray says this: "Just as water seeks and fills the lowest place, so the moment God finds the creature empty, His glory and power flow in to exalt and to bless. He that humbles himself—that must be our one aim—shall be exalted; that is God's aim. By His mighty power and in His great love He will do it."[1]

When we live with our hearts low, assuming a position of wor-ship, God comes into our now and takes care of everything, exactly where we need Him. Including lifting us up when He decides to. James 4:10 confirms this: "Humble yourselves before the Lord, and he will lift you up."

Humility is powerful. It also positions us as worshipers, always ascribing worth to the only One who loves us unconditionally. (The world sure doesn't!) And it kicks the devil's behind. Look at what comes right after the verse that tells us God gives grace to the humble: "Submit yourselves, then, to God. Resist the devil, and he will flee from you" (James 4:7).

As we walk in humble submission to God, He gives us His grace to resist the pull and temptations of the world, and to resist the lies and distractions that we face every day . . . and the devil can't stand it. He runs away, leaving us to bask in God's presence and truth.

PREVENTATIVE MEASURE #2: OBEDIENCE

The two most powerful characteristics we see in the life of Christ are humility and obedience. In fact, I believe it was these two things that, in great measure, were responsible for His earthly displays of victory and power.

When Jesus was here on earth, the Bible tells us He chose not to tap into His divine power. Rather, He humbled Himself and lived as a man—an obedient, Spirit-led man. And what's so wonderful about that is, when we see what He did and how He did it, we know there's at least a chance we can do it too. There's no way we can be perfect like God in heaven, but we can at least hope to emulate a perfect human, especially with the power of the Holy Spirit working in us.

We know that Jesus humbled Himself, not only by putting on humanity, but also by suffering and dying for us. But how can we be sure He walked in obedience? Well, because He said so. "Jesus said to them, 'Very truly I tell you, the Son can do nothing by himself; he can do only what he sees his Father doing, because whatever the Father does the Son also does'" (John 5:19).

Jesus didn't do anything of His own accord. He did what the Father told Him to do—and what He saw the Father doing. And because of it, His earthly life was fruitful and free. Jesus had the healthiest personal boundaries of any human being to ever live.

No people-pleasing there! Just Father-pleasing. And His obedience saved mankind.

Is our obedience powerful too? Yes, it is.

If you want to know what happens when God's children choose not to obey, just take a look at the experiences of the Israelites. There were many consequences they could have avoided if they'd only obeyed. And God was always faithful to warn them over and over.

God warns us to obey because He knows all the benefits it brings us. He has fashioned things so that when we obey Him, our lives go as they should and bring about His desired results (which are the best ones). What's more, He knows that obedience is good for our soul. It's good for our mind, will, and even our emotions.

Look at 1 Peter 1:22 in the ESV: "Having purified your souls *by your obedience* to the truth for a sincere brotherly love, love one another earnestly from a pure heart." Obedience to the truth purifies our souls. Who wouldn't want a pure soul? Who wouldn't want to feel clean and new and refreshed? I sure do. When we obey God, supernatural things like this happen inside of us. Transformation happens.

Obedience is like a key. Every time we obey, we unlock a treasure chest. Sometimes what we get is huge amounts of healing or years of reaping wiped away in an instant. Sometimes it's not that dramatic, but the joy of knowing we've done the right thing before the Lord, along with the absence of guilt and emotional heaviness, is so life-giving.

What keeps us from doing this all the time if it's so amazing? Don't you think it's usually fear? We're afraid to let go of something, or afraid of the unknown. You see, when we obey, it's like saying, *I choose You, God.* We are casting our lot with Him. But at that very moment, we also have to say we *don't* want the thing we're turning away from, and that's not always easy.

It's not always easy because that *thing* we're rejecting might be all we've ever known. Even though we don't like the feel of it anymore, it's what we've grown accustomed to, like an old, dirty coat. We know it's ugly, but it fits, and it's all we have in hand at the moment.

We settle for far less than we're meant to. Yet God offers us so much more!

When God asks us to trust and follow Him, it's because He has something far better for us than we can imagine. And when we really get to the bottom of it all, the better thing He has for us is . . . Himself. Authors Roy and Revel Hession write: "The glorious truth is that He is Himself not only the way to blessing but the needed blessing itself; not only the way to power but our power; not only the way to victory but our victory; not only the way to sanctification but our sanctification; not only the way to healing but our healing; not only the way to revival but our revival; and so on for everything else."[2]

Scripture implores us: "Taste and see that the LORD is good; blessed is the one who takes refuge in him" (Psalm 34:8). We might think we need a better job, a new house, more provisions, or some special calling. But what we really need is the Provider of all those things. And the way we learn this—the way we taste and see for ourselves—is to trust Him enough to relinquish our desire for what doesn't last, even if it's just one thing at a time. We have to be brave enough to let God fill that place with Himself alone.

We will never know whether He is good until we try. But once we try, we'll want to keep at it again and again because having our deepest needs met by God is what we're made for.

PREVENTATIVE MEASURE #3: A LITTLE R & R

Remember when we were little and something was wrong with our hair, or there was dirt on our face, and our mom wanted to straighten us out? She'd hold our arms and say, "Stand still!" and then she'd lick her thumb and clean us up (something I swore I'd never do to my kids, but . . . well, I'm guilty).

Sometimes I think I hear God saying that too. When things are all out of whack, and I've lost my way, I hear Him say, "Be still, and know that I am God" (Psalm 46:10a).

Just like Mom couldn't help us out much when we were wiggling all over the place, God knows that His Spirit works best in a captive audience. I think that's why the Bible has so much to say about rest.

The Quakers, who also refer to themselves as Friends, place a high value upon rest and silence. In fact, they have entire worship services comprised of nothing but silence. Imagine an hour or more of sitting together in a quiet room, expectantly waiting for God to show up!

Silence is where Quakers believe they encounter the real presence of Christ. They don't have rites or symbols, or use bread or wine. The silence is their Communion service. According to J. Brent Bill, "Quakers see holy silence as so crucial to Christianity that we can't contemplate faith without it. It is crucial to the life of faith."[3]

Although I'd never make a great Quaker, I admire their devotion to times of silence. Probably because it's such a challenge for me. Even when I do sit down for quiet time, I have to wrangle my own thoughts to the ground. *Okay, Teasi, be quiet. For real this time. Stop talking. But don't forget to get milk today, okay? Yes . . . just be quiet. Okay, I'm getting quiet now. How much time do I have left?*

Silence and rest have to be practiced. And the more we practice them, the more fruit we will see. For one, we will find it much easier to keep the main thing the main thing. We won't be so easily fooled by the lure of *bigger* and *better*—that productivity trap we see all around us. We will know that our salvation and our satisfaction are not found in accomplishing more but in resting. Resting in the arms of the One who longs to have us all to Himself.

God tried to tell His people this truth when they kept trusting in worldly power and position. Look at what He says in Isaiah 30:15a: "In returning and rest you shall be saved; in quietness and trust shall be your strength" (ESV). In repentance (returning to Him) and in rest we shall be saved. In quietness (not in platform-building and networking) will be our strength.

When we feel the old, familiar longing for a *big calling* start creeping back in again—maybe because we see everyone making a big deal about some speaker at a conference or some Christian celebrity on a talk show—we know we need some rest. When we start wishing someone would finally recognize our unique gifts and abilities, we need some rest. When we feel like we're losing our peace and our joy, we need some rest.

In our quiet, restful times with the Father, He will remind us of what matters most, and He will help us remember that wherever He is, there is majesty.

FINDING MAJESTY IN THE MUNDANE

There truly is majesty in the mundane.

I'd like to share a Quaker poem that shows it so beautifully. If you're like me, you might be tempted to skip it, but please don't. Read it slowly, and really let it sink in.

Holy as a Day Is Spent

Holy is the dish and drain
The soap and sink, and the cup and plate
And the warm wool socks, and cold white tile
Showerheads and good dry towels
And frying eggs sound like psalms
With a bit of salt measured in my palm
It's all a part of a sacrament
As holy as a day is spent

Holy is the busy street
And cars that boom with passion's beat
And the checkout girl, counting change
And the hands that shook my hands today

And hymns of geese fly overhead
And stretch their wings like their parents did
Blessed be the dog, that runs in her sleep
To catch that wild and elusive thing

Holy is the familiar room
And the quiet moments in the afternoon
And folding sheets like folding hands
To pray as only laundry can
I'm letting go of all I fear
Like autumn leaves of earth and air
For summer came and summer went
As holy as a day is spent

Holy is the place I stand
To give whatever small good I can
And the empty page, and the open book
Redemption everywhere I look
Unknowingly we slow our pace
In the shade of unexpected grace
And with grateful smiles and sad lament
As holy as a day is spent
And morning light sings "providence"
As holy as a day is spent

———

Carrie Newcomer[4]

Try to find the majesty in everything just for one day. Invite your children to join you if you have little ones living at home. They're actually quite good at it.

Right after I read that poem for the first time, that's exactly what I did. And it worked. I was undone by the love of God as

I began to see Him in places I never would have before. I saw the familiar strands of runaway hairs in my bathroom sink and thought: *God knows just how many of these fell out this morning . . . and He knows precisely how many are left on my head. Thank You, Father, for knowing me so well.*

I saw a million dust particles floating around in the light of my living room window and I reminded myself: *The Father's thoughts toward me are more numerous than these floaters. He is constantly thinking good things about me.*

I folded a load of towels and reflected: *These towels are bending—humbly folded in on themselves, just as my Savior humbled Himself for me. Thank You, Jesus, for taking my place on that cross.*

The majestic found me right where I was, and it can find you. It might not change the circumstances of the day, and it probably won't do the dishes for you. But it will change you on the inside if you let it.

"The fullness of Christian life can be lived anywhere, in any circumstance, because God is with us," declares Skye Jethani. "No condition of life is more honorable than another, because nothing God does lacks value. If He is with us in marriage or singleness, and in the garage, the office, or the home, then these very different lives are each significant. Each of them carries the same dignity and hope."[5]

ONE MORE THING BEFORE YOU GO

God is so good. And the world needs to know it.

We get to show them.

Isn't it an incredible honor? You and me, we're here to help people find the Remedy, the Truth, and real Life. That's something to hold our heads high about. It's a role no one can take and no evil can shake. It's the safest place to find our value, our hope, our destiny. Let's never let go of this truth.

I'd like to leave you with a prayer that helps me keep the first thing first. I'd like to share it with you—for you to take it and make it your own if you'd like.

Would you pray it with me before you go?

Father,

I love You and thank You for the endless love You lavish on me. Thank You for the amazing reason for which I exist. Thank You that I wasn't born into a purposeless life filled with purposeless days leading to an uncertain future. Thank You that I can trust You, and that You've called me Your own.

Forgive me, Father, for the times I've longed for everything but You. For the times I've wanted You only for what You can give me or do for me rather than simply for who You are. I don't want to do that anymore. I can see that all those things are mere counterfeits, unable to compare to the greatness of who You are and the beauty of Your presence. In Your presence I am made whole. In Your presence is fullness of joy. Help me to stay there.

Father, I ask You to lead me in a new path—one of purpose first, leaving my callings up to You. Help me to learn exactly

*how You've designed me in order to bring You the most glory,
because in this way, I am helping the blind to see. I am helping
the hurting find the Healer, and the lost their true Home.*

*Let me know You more and more each day and see You in places
I've never seen You before. I want to see You on earth, Lord, as I
anticipate that beautiful day when I can see You face to face.*

*I choose this day to enjoy the beautiful area rug You've
handstitched for me. Don't let me miss one single, colorful
thread. And if ever You decide to take me on a flying carpet
ride, I'll just hold on tight and enjoy the experience.*

I love You, and I am Yours.

Eternally,

Your Beloved Glorifier

HOW ABOUT YOU?

1) What does it mean to you to "be nothing" in this quote
from Andrew Murray? "Nothing is more natural and beautiful and blessed than to be nothing in order that God may
be everything."[6]

2) What, if anything, has God asked you to do lately that you've hesitated about? What do you think is stopping you from obeying?

3) How much quiet time do you get each week—meaning, time when you're not even reading or praying but just sitting in the silence with God? Do you feel this is enough time?

4) What do you think of this Quaker saying: "Busyness is moral laziness"? According to this standard, would you be considered lazy or hardworking?

POINTS ON PURPOSE:

» God has given us some preventative medicine to help us avoid catching the special-calling bug. Our best plan of prevention includes humility, obedience, repentance, and rest. If we make these a regular part of life, we will stay the course with joy.

» The more we live our lives with our primary purpose at the center, the more we will begin to glimpse the divine in the daily, the amazing in the ordinary. What used to be merely the mundane will become the very best places to see the majesty of the One who is truly our all.

ACKNOWLEDGMENTS

I'm so thankful God places us in families, because I can't imagine what I'd do without mine. My husband, Bill, and our three children—Carli, Ben, and Sam—are the sweetest gifts (other than salvation) that God has given me. I can't thank them enough for their loving support, prayers, and comic relief throughout the process of writing this book. My incredible parents, multitalented sister, charismatic brother (celebrating in heaven), and extraordinary extended family are also due my endless gratitude. I love you all and thank you for always loving me.

I'm also grateful that God gives us friends, and boy, do I have some great ones! I could write an additional book full of nothing but praises for the amazing, talented, loving, and faithful buddies God has placed in my life since my earliest days. But for now I will simply say thank you to all of you who have called me friend.

I'm thankful for my Grace Chapel family—pastors, counselors, and all my siblings in Christ. I've spent nearly half my life growing with this faithful warrior tribe, and I praise God for every single thing I've gleaned as one of your members.

And I thank God for the people who very specifically helped me in the production of this book. First, Kris Bearss. Your friendship, encouragement, wisdom, and of course, editorial and project-management expertise, are a priceless gift to me. I really can't thank you and your amazing team enough. Wayne Hastings, thank you for your kind support and seasoned advice pertaining to all things publishing. Joanne Kraft, thank you so much for your friendship, inspiration, and encouraging nudges to get these words on paper.

Thank you to all the generous friends who took their time to read the manuscript in order to give endorsements or feedback: Marsha Gootee (mom), Pastor Steve Berger, Tammy Trent, Jo Dee Messina, Dave Buehring, Steve Craver, Nancy Reece, Toni Birdsong, Allison Allen, Adie Camp, Joanne Kraft, and my sweet husband, Bill, who lets me read every single word out loud to him. I appreciate each and every one of you more than I can say.

And, of course, to the very reason I live: Father, Son, and Holy Spirit. I thank You, great and mighty God, with my whole heart. I want nothing more than to glorify You with my life and with my words. I submit this book to You as an offering of praise. I love You . . . forever.

RECOMMENDED READING

(as promised in Chapter 7)

BOOKS:

Geisler, Norman and Frank Turek. *I Don't Have Enough Faith to Be an Atheist.* Wheaton, IL: Crossway, 2004.

Habermas, Gary and Michael Licona. *The Case for the Resurrection of Jesus.* Grand Rapids, MI: Kregel Publications, 2004.

Koukl, Gregory. *The Story of Reality: How the World Began, How It Ends, and Everything in Between.* Grand Rapids, MI: Zondervan, 2017.

Lewis, C. S. *Mere Christianity.* New York: HarperCollins, 2002.

Qureshi, Nabeel. *No God but One: Allah or Jesus?* Grand Rapids, MI: Zondervan, 2016.

Strobel, Lee. *The Case for Christ.* Grand Rapids, MI: Zondervan, 2016.

Wallace, J. Warner. *Cold-Case Christianity.* Colorado Springs, CO: David C. Cook, 2013.

Zacharias, Ravi. *Why Jesus? Rediscovering His Truth in an Age of Mass Marketed Spirituality.* New York: Hachette, 2012.

WEBSITES:

Stand to Reason: *http://www.str.org/*

Cross Examined: *http://crossexamined.org/*

J. Warner Wallace and Cold-Case Christianity: *http://coldcasechristianity.com/*

Ravi Zacharias: *http://rzim.org/*

NOTES

CHAPTER 2: WEBSTER TO THE RESCUE

1. J. P. Moreland, *Love Your God with All Your Mind: The Role of Reason in the Life of the Soul* (Colorado Springs, CO: NavPress, 1997), 86.

2. William Lane Craig, *Hard Questions, Real Answers* (Wheaton, IL: Crossway, 2003), 94.

3. Ravi Zacharias, *Grand Weaver: How God Shapes Us through the Events of Our Lives* (Grand Rapids, MI: Zondervan, 2007), 132.

4. Andrew Murray, *The Believer's Secret to Waiting on God* (Minneapolis: Bethany House, 1986), 23.

CHAPTER 3: WHY THEM?

1. Ravi Zacharias, *Grand Weaver: How God Shapes Us through the Events of Our Lives* (Grand Rapids, MI: Zondervan, 2007), 37.

2. Ravi Zacharias, *Recapture the Wonder* (Nashville: Thomas Nelson, 2003), 125.

CHAPTER 4: OPPORTUNITY COST

1. Neil Anderson, *Victory Over the Darkness: Realizing the Power of Your Identity in Christ* (Ventura, CA: Regal Books, 2000), 131.

2. Ibid., 132.

3. Skye Jethani, *With: Reimagining the Way You Relate to God* (Nashville: Thomas Nelson, 2011), 150.

4. Roy and Revel Hession, *We Would See Jesus: Discovering God's Provision for You in Christ* (Fort Washington, PA: CLC Publications, 1958), 123.

CHAPTER 5: A DO-DO MENTALITY

1. John Burke, *Imagine Heaven: Near-Death Experiences. God's Promises, and the Exhilarating Future That Awaits You* (Grand Rapids, MI: Baker Books, 2015), 72.

2. J. Warner Wallace, *Cold-Case Christianity: A Homicide Detective Investigates the Claims of the Gospels* (Colorado Springs, CO: David C. Cook, 2013).

3. Ravi Zacharias, *Grand Weaver: How God Shapes Us through the Events of Our Lives* (Grand Rapids, MI: Zondervan, 2007), 55.

CHAPTER 6: IS *CALLING* IN THE BIBLE?

1. Ravi Zacharias, *Grand Weaver: How God Shapes Us through the Events of Our Lives* (Grand Rapids, MI: Zondervan, 2007), 64.

2. Roy and Revel Hession, *We Would See Jesus: Discovering God's Provision for You in Christ* (Fort Washington, PA: CLC Publications, 1958), 122.

CHAPTER 7: WHAT'S SO GREAT ABOUT PURPOSE?

1. Richard Dawkins, *The Blind Watchmaker* (New York: Norton, 1987), 17–18, 116.

CHAPTER 8: PURPOSE YOUR WAY

1. John Burke, *Imagine Heaven: Near-Death Experiences, God's Promises, and the Exhilarating Future That Awaits You* (Grand Rapids, MI: Baker Books, 2015), 78.

2. J. P. Moreland, *Love Your God with All Your Mind: The Role of Reason in the Life of the Soul* (Colorado Springs, CO: NavPress, 1997), 175.

3. Skye Jethani, *With: Reimagining the Way You Relate to God* (Nashville: Thomas Nelson, 2011), 151.

CHAPTER 9: LIKE AN AREA RUG

1. "The Fatherless Generation: Statistics"; https://thefatherless generation.wordpress.com/statistics/.

2. Joseph Castro, "How a Mother's Love Changes a Child's Brain" (January 30, 2012); http://www.livescience.com/18196-maternal -support-child-brain.html.

3. "What is the 'Pareto Principle,'" http://www.investopedia.com/terms/p/paretoprinciple.asp.

4. Ravi Zacharias, *Grand Weaver: How God Shapes Us Through the Events of Our Lives* (Grand Rapids, MI: Zondervan, 2007), 61.

5. Ibid., 58.

CHAPTER 10: PURPOSEFULLY EVER AFTER

1. Andrew Murray, *Humility: The Journey Toward Holiness* (Bloomington, MN: Bethany House, 2001), 41.

2. Roy and Revel Hession, *We Would See Jesus: Discovering God's Provision for You in Christ.* (Fort Washington, PA: CLC Publications, 1958), 129.

3. J. Brent Bill, *Holy Silence: The Gift of Quaker Spirituality* (Brewster, MA: Paraclete Press, 2006), 48.

4. Ibid., 29.

5. Skye Jethani, *With: Reimagining the Way You Relate to God* (Nashville: Thomas Nelson, 2012), 152.

6. Andrew Murray, *Humility: The Journey toward Holiness* (Bloomington, MN: Bethany House, 2001), 10.

TEASI CANNON has a master's in pastoral counseling from Liberty Theological Seminary and is a Bible teacher and sought-after retreat speaker. The author of *My Big Bottom Blessing: How Hating My Body Led to Loving My Life* (Worthy Publishing), she has been featured on numerous radio and television shows, and she blogs occasionally. Teasi and her husband, Bill, have three children: Carli, Ben, and Sam.

Wheaton Press
Train. Equip. Reflect.

JOIN THE CONVERSATION...

- Head over to facebook.com/teasicannon, click "LIKE," and post a comment regarding what you enjoyed about the book

- Recommend the book to your friends on social media

- Post a review online

- Discover more resources to equip you in your journey and connect with social media at WheatonPress.com/TeasiCannon

INVITE TEASI TO YOUR EVENT

A respected speaker, teacher, and writer, Teasi brings an inspired message of vision, healing, and biblical freedom.

• • • • • • • • • • • • • **WHAT OTHERS ARE SAYING** • • • • • • • • • • • • •

"I do not hesitate to recommend Teasi Cannon. She possesses a winsome vulnerability that softens hearts, and then she drops in the rich seed of the Word with skill. Truly, she exalts Christ."

• • • • • • • •

Dee Brestin, author of *The Friendships of Women,*
Falling in Love with Jesus, and *Idol Lies*

"Teasi surpassed our high standards! I can certainly attest to Teasi's very gifted, highly relational, witty, and scripturally solid presentation."

• • • • • • • •

Dawn Bodi, "Put Your Brave On" Women's Retreat

"We loved Teasi! She was exactly what we were looking for. She fit perfectly into our retreat goals!"

• • • • • • • •

Sara Rupp, Miracle Camp Retreat Center

WP *Wheaton Press*
Train. Equip. Reflect.

LEARN MORE AT WHEATONPRESS.COM/TEASICANNON

Made in the USA
Middletown, DE
09 July 2020